The Open University

Technology: A Foundation Course

Living with Technology

Block 1
Home

Prepared by the Course Team

The Open University Press

The Open University, Walton Hall, Milton Keynes.

First published 1988.
Reprinted 1990, 1991 and 1992.

Designed by the Graphic Design Group of the Open University.

Typeset in the UK by Speedlith Photo Litho Limited, Longford Trading Estate, Thomas Street, Stretford, Manchester M32 0JT.

Printed and bound in the UK by Staples Printers Rochester Limited, Neptune Close, Medway City Estate, Frindsbury, Rochester, Kent ME2 4LT.

ISBN 0 335 17335 7

This text forms part of the correspondence element of an Open University Foundation Course.

For general availability of supporting material referred to in this text, please write to Open University Educational Enterprises Limited, 12 Cofferidge Close, Stony Stratford, Milton Keynes MK11 1BY, UK.

Further information on Open University courses may be obtained from The Admissions Office, The Open University, P.O. Box 48, Walton Hall, Milton Keynes MK7 6AB.

Contents

Throughout Block 1 *Home* you will find 'study notes' like this one printed in blue. The purpose of these notes is to help you to study effectively, that is, to help your learning process.

Reading

You will have to read many thousands of words in this course. Your time is clearly limited, and it pays to think about how you might read with speed and efficiency to achieve your study goals.

Usually to 'read' means only one kind of reading: to start with the first word of a book or article and to progress from left to right, line by line through each and every page until the end is finally reached. But this is only one kind of reading, and it serves only one kind of purpose. Often you won't *need* to read every word of a book or article. You may be looking for a particular detail, fact or reference, or you may just want to get the flavour or scope of a book, to see whether it is worth your while to spend more time on it. Each of these purposes needs a different reading strategy. Think of your *purpose* in reading, and the kind of strategy needed will usually suggest itself. If you follow this advice, you will save yourself a great deal of time, and you won't have to work through a lot of exercises to improve your reading speed. But do remember that each of the teaching texts in a course like *Living with Technology* has been specially and carefully prepared to guide your study through complex subjects; you won't find much that is superfluous and can be skipped.

Now I suggest you practise one of these reading strategies. You have just picked up Block 1 *Home* and it will form one of your main sources of study material for the next five weeks. But before starting to read the first words of this book, *survey* it:

try to find your way around it,

get the flavour of it,

find out what issues it deals with.

Here are some ways of doing this:

Look back at the 'Contents' page.

What are the main topics?

Which of these are dealt with at length?

How are the topics grouped (e.g. in what order)?

Flick through the pages. Pause to look at anything that interests you. Look at illustrations, diagrams and tables as well as at headings.

Look at the section introductions and summaries. These contain the main ideas of each section.

This survey need take only about ten minutes, though you can spend more time if you wish. The important thing is to get an idea of the structure of the block. To get this overall picture of the block's organization will give you a framework into which you can fit the details later, when you study each section. To browse through also helps your motivation: you will be looking forward to studying the interesting sections later.

You should begin your study of Block 1 *Home* by reading (or re-reading) the 'Study guide to Block 1'. Then read on.

Note taking

Note taking is one of the most important skills and one that you will need to practise again and again, not only in this course but in all your studies with the Open University. In Block 1 these study notes will introduce various ideas on how to write and to organize your notes.

Exercise

This exercise (based on what you read in the 'Study guide to Block 1') is intended to set you thinking about what is involved in taking notes. Using the space below to jot down your notes, answer the following question as briefly as you like. Try to answer it in note form, without looking back to the 'Study guide to Block 1'.

What will you be learning by working through Block 1 'Home'?

When you have written your notes (which shouldn't take you more than ten minutes) compare them with those in the 'discussion', below.

Discussion

A typical answer might be:

About the technology of houses and of my own home.

Some basic principles of technology.

About 'design' – awareness of it and some practice in it.
Basic skills – e.g. in numeracy and studying.

About the basic principles of operating my computer and running the Framework program.

Now check back to the Study Guide and see if your notes, and the ones above, seem to be on the right lines.

Here are three things to remember when you are taking notes:

1 *Notes should have a purpose*

For example, in the case of the notes you have just written, the purposes were:

to give you some practice in writing notes, and a chance to think about what is involved in that process;

to help you to grasp some important points from the 'Study guide', to make sure that some key intentions of the Course Team would not pass you by.

2 *Notes should help you to learn*

This point is often forgotten by students. It's all too easy to take pages of notes and to convince yourself that this means that you are working. Note taking should be a process involving thoughtful alertness, not a substitute for real work.

3 *Notes should be personal to you*

Good notes are the notes you take to help you to satisfy your own particular purposes. Notes should, as far as possible, be *in your own words* because this makes it more likely that you will have *thought* about the ideas. You will be translating them through your own mind and expressing them in your own way. You will, in fact, be learning.

It's a good idea to have a notebook in which you keep all your study notes as you work through the course material. Use it for recording important terms that the authors use, defining them in your own words so that you understand them, and for making diagrams and your other study notes.

Part One Simple shelter

1 Simple traditional houses

Some peoples of the world do not build houses for themselves, or indeed shelters of any kind beyond an occasional wind-break. But these are a very few exceptions; almost every tribe, nation or race throughout the world and throughout history builds and has built houses. A house, or at least simple shelter of some kind, therefore seems to be a basic technology that just about everybody wants.

But everybody also, so it seems, has their own peculiar ideas about what 'a house' is: how big it should be, what shape it should have, with which materials it should be made, and so on. Examples of traditional houses from around the world exhibit an extraordinary diversity, which suggests that what modern Europeans take for granted as being 'a house' is only one peculiarity. No doubt we can learn something about our own attitudes and requirements from an awareness of *other* people's peculiarities.

Throughout most of history people have not really needed to be taught about the technology of their houses. The basic need for a house has been so important and pervasive that everyone could design and build their own, perhaps with a little help from their friends. But in Western industrialized society this knowledge that everyone once had has increasingly become the specialized knowledge of a few.

If you are not one of these specialists, then perhaps, at a pinch, you *could* still manage to design and build a house of sorts, but it is likely to be rather a crude effort. Think of the kind of mistakes you are likely to make:

You might find that the building materials you try to use are not really suitable for what you want to do.

You might find that the house collapses easily, that it lacks stability.

You might find that it lets in the damp, or is not warm enough, not light enough inside, or not big enough.

You might find the house unsuitable in particular conditions: say in a heavy downpour of rain, in a high wind, or on very hot days.

You might find it inconvenient: the door is in the wrong place, or the rooms are the wrong shape, or the windows could face in better directions.
(Even specialists can make these kinds of mistakes.)

All these things, and many more, you would discover during your building and living in the house. By gradual trial and error you would probably improve the house over time, but it would be a very slow learning process. After many years' experience you might be able to pass on to other people a few good tips about the designing and building of a house. That handing on of tips and advice is the way that craft knowledge passed from generation to generation in earlier societies. It worked well as an educational system provided that everyone built more or less the same kind of house, using more or less the same kind of materials, and lived in it in more or less the same kind of way.

In modern society the informal passing on of craft knowledge from one generation to the next has been largely superseded by a more formalized education system, which, particularly at university level, is much more concerned with the teaching and learning of basic principles than the passing on of apparently unchangeable facts. So, although this block seems to be about a fairly practical subject, you will find that you are being asked to learn principles rather than to remember facts.

Curiously, one of the best ways of learning some of the principles involved in house design is to begin by looking at houses that are, or were, built in the craft tradition that has now nearly disappeared from our society.

So here I shall briefly review a dozen or so examples of simple traditional, or 'vernacular', houses from around the world. Already my Western attitudes are showing in the use of the word 'simple' to categorize these buildings. As you will see, traditional design and technology is usually considerably skilful, ingenious and appropriate, as well as often carrying religious, social or other symbolic meaning. In my choice of examples I shall concentrate on the houses that are found as common types in given societies.

Yurt

The yurt is a tent form used for thousands of years by nomadic tribes in central Asia. It is easily transported and quickly erected. The vertical sides of the yurt are formed by light timber panels of a kind of trellis-work, which can be folded and unfolded very easily. These are arranged to form a circular enclosure, completed by a wooden door and frame. The roof is of light timber struts loosely fastened to a large ring. This ring forms the apex of the roof, with the struts making a dome-like roof structure. The whole framework is then covered with layers of felt sheets, the number of layers depending on the severity of the weather. Although apparently 'simple', the yurt is a clever design solution to the problem of providing a house that can be carried on one or two camels, using the rather sparse building materials available in the region.

Figure 1   A yurt in the process of erection

Igloo

Igloo is an Eskimo word for 'house'. Although we usually only associate the word with snow-houses, the Eskimo also traditionally build houses using timber and earth. The snow-house is a temporary shelter built on hunting trips, and is erected quite quickly. It is made from snow blocks cut to rather subtle curved and wedged shapes. The blocks are built up in a continuous spiral to form the familiar hemispherical igloo dome. Beside the main living dome, the igloo has a tunnelled entry-passage, with a subsidiary room or rooms attached to it. The entry is protected from the wind by a wall, and the entry-passage is itself usually curved to prevent direct draughts entering the main room. The interior may be lined with skins and furs, supported from toggle fastenings let into the domed roof. With fairly minimal heating from an oil lamp the interior temperature is comfortable (for an Eskimo) despite the Arctic climate, staying at around 0 °C even when the outside temperature may be − 15°C. Three or four igloos may be built around, and leading from, a large communal room, used for dancing and other ceremonies.

Figure 2   Ceremonial drum-dance igloo, Tuktoyaktuk, North-West Territories, Canada

Grass house

In many regions of the world a light grass house is the only form of shelter required, just as a light grass skirt is the only form of clothing. Typically, walls are an open frame of light timber poles supporting a roof frame that is thatched with grass. The walls may also be filled in with thatching, or hung with grass matting. The main sheltering function of the house is simply to provide shade from the sun.

Pueblo

The term *pueblo* is Spanish for 'town', but it is used in English to refer both to the native peoples (actually of several different tribes) and to their buildings, located in the south-west desert regions of North America. A pueblo house is made of thick mud walls with a flat roof of mud on timber poles. The houses are built in multi-storeyed, stepped terraces, arranged around an open plaza. The multi-storeyed, stepped structure creates a honeycomb of interior rooms at the lower levels; these rooms are used for storage. The upper storeys are reached by ladders, and open onto the flat roofs of the storeys below. These flat roofs are used as places for sitting out, for domestic work and also for sleeping. A heavy form of construction like this acts like a kind of storage heater: it slowly absorbs the heat of the sun during the day, and then slowly releases it again to the occupants' benefit during the cold night.

Figure 3   Two examples of African grass houses

Figure 4   Part of a pueblo terrace, Taos, New Mexico, USA

Tepee

The familiar American Indian tepee consists of a covering of buffalo hides over a conical structure of timber poles. An opening at the top allows smoke to escape and light to enter, but it can be closed by the flaps attached to separate poles. These flaps can also be positioned and directed to catch the breeze and so ventilate the tepee. Like most tents the tepee is relatively easily dismantled, moved and reassembled, a necessary feature of shelter for nomads such as the American Plains Indians.

Figure 5
Tepees

Trullo

In and around the small town of Alberobello in Apulia, Italy, the traditional house is known as a *trullo* (plural: *trulli*). This is a small house of thick stone walls and a conical stone roof. The stone used is the very abundant local limestone, laid entirely dry (i.e. without mortar) in both walls and roof. Great skill is necessary to construct such dry-stone buildings, especially the hollow roof cone. A *trullo* house might typically have one main room, with large alcoves or semi-enclosed rooms off. Beneath the main room there is often a basement cistern for storing water. The ceiling vault is built up in concentric rings of roughly trimmed stones, each ring projecting inwards a little farther than the one below. A single large stone eventually closes the roof at its top, and it is sometimes capped with a decorative pinnacle. The outside of the roof is slated with flat stones, and the walls are often plastered and whitewashed a brilliant white.

Figure 6
Trulli

Forest pavilion

The traditional house in tropical forest regions of the world (such as parts of Africa, Asia and South America) is often little more than an open-sided pavilion. A frame of timber poles supports a light thatched roof and the timber floor, which might be raised about a metre above the ground. This raised floor allows adequate ventilation and cooling breezes to circulate in the hot, humid climate and provides protection against animals, insects and floods. The steeply sloping and overhanging roof provides shade from the hot sun and serves as an umbrella against the torrential rain. The sides of the house can be left entirely open, so as to allow whatever ventilation may be possible, or closed in with walls of bark or grass matting. This kind of house is well-suited to the climatic conditions in which the inhabitants live.

Figure 7   Forest pavilions: (a) a Melanesian village on the Trobriand Isles, South Pacific; (b) near Iquitos, Peru

(a)

(b)

Mandan lodge

The Mandan Indians of the upper Missouri regions of the USA lived traditionally in a circular lodge housing five or six families. The lodge was about ten metres in diameter, constructed essentially of a timber frame covered with earth and turf. The walls were of timber poles leaning against a supporting framework and covered on the outside by earth blocks, which were in turn covered with turf. The wall frame and an inner framework supported the roof rafters, which were covered with grass matting and turf. A central hole in the roof let out the smoke of the fireplace and also admitted light. This hole could be covered with buffalo skin to keep out rain. Buffalo skins also provided interior partitions and a means of closing the doorway.

Bedouin tent

The Bedouin people are principally nomadic shepherds, living in the Arabian desert regions. Sheep and goats provide the Bedouin livelihood, and these animals have to be moved from place to place to take advantage of the rather sparse areas of vegetation for their grazing. The tent therefore provides a readily demountable and transportable form of shelter. The roof and walls of the Bedouin 'black tent' are sheets of woven black goats' hair or sheep's wool or both. The roof is supported by a simple framework of timber poles, secured and made rigid by guy-ropes. Side and interior curtains are placed so as to enclose and divide the tent (e.g. into men's and women's quarters) and to exclude or to catch the wind. The long guy-ropes also provide support for draping the curtains in various arrangements to create semi-enclosed areas and wind-breaks.

Figure 8   A Mandan lodge

Figure 9   A 'black tent' of the Bedouin

Dogon house

The Dogon people live along the Bandiagara plateau south of Timbuktu in Mali, Africa. They build their villages at the foot of cliffs and rock outcrops. Each family house, with its store rooms, granaries and stables, is built as a cluster of rooms around a courtyard. The walls are built from mud bricks, plastered with a mixture of clay and straw. The house has a flat clay roof on a framework of timber beams, whereas the store rooms and granaries are usually roofed with cones of thatch. The flat roofs, reached by a

Figure 10   (below and opposite) Two views of Dogon houses

notched tree-trunk ladder, are used for sleeping during the hottest months of the year. The Dogon people have a very complex pattern of symbolic meanings attaching to their houses and all other aspects of their environment. A Dogon house plan is on page 14.

Figure 11   Archetypal English cottages

English cottage

The archetypal English house is probably the small, black and white, thatched cottage with roses around the door, etc. The now black-painted timbers (which were originally unpainted) are the structural supporting frame of the house, with the walling between being usually of 'wattle and daub'. This consists of clay daubed onto an infill made of thin, pliable sticks interwoven something like basketwork and known as wattle. The clay daub is finished with a plaster coating. The thick roof covering of thatch is made of straw or reeds. Again this vernacular house-type is well-suited to the prevailing climate (providing a warm, dry enclosure) and uses the available materials to best advantage.

2 Some reasons for diversity

Why are simple traditional houses around the world so diverse in their forms, sizes, shapes, materials, etc? The variety of solutions to the basic need for a shelter seems to be much greater than the variety of human types. If, 'under the skin', all people are very similar, why do they come to such different design solutions for their houses?

Exercise

To ensure that you are reading and studying actively, prepare your own thoughts for what you would expect to be coming now in this section. Try writing a few notes in the space below suggesting some reasons for the great variety of houses built all over the world. Spend five to ten minutes on this. *Don't* look ahead to the rest of this section until you have written your notes in the space below.

This exercise is a way of helping you to approach the block *actively*. The great danger in studying is to remain passive, but if you can compare your own ideas with the author's, then you will be in a questioning mood.

Some of the readily identifiable and principal reasons for the prodigal diversity of people's houses are:

(a) People build with *materials* that are close at hand, and these materials vary from region to region: from stone to snow and from earth to timber.

(b) *Climates* vary regionally, and impose different requirements on the basic shelter, such as keeping out cold, or heat, or wet.

(c) People have different *ways of life*: some people are nomadic shepherds or hunters, some are settled farmers, some are fishermen, etc.

(d) Levels of *technological knowledge and skill* vary between different peoples (compare, say, the Ancient Britons with their Roman invaders), and at different periods.

(e) There are different *economic constraints* operating in different societies and even between different groups of people within the same society.

(f) People have different *social and cultural habits and traditions*, such as living communally or separately, they have different religious, ethical and moral attitudes, they invest their houses with symbolic meanings, and so on.

Materials

Clearly, the available materials have an important influence on what kind of house can be built. In most societies there has not been the great choice of materials that transport and manufacturing industries make available to modern Western society. Usually a house builder has to gather materials from a fairly small locality, for example, the trullo builder picks his stones from his fields, or the builder has rather limited resources, for example the Bedouin have to rely on the hair and wool of their goats and sheep. This limitation of materials imposes limits on what *can* be built; for instance, it is difficult to build a large flat roof with just snow as your material. But it is also clear that some materials can be used to build a variety of different forms: mud roofs can be flat, domed, sloping, etc.

Climate

Climate is often regarded as *the* most important factor influencing traditional house design. Even the common use of the word 'shelter' to indicate the basic function of a house betrays this emphasis. However, climate can really only be regarded as one (albeit important) factor among many that make up the total pattern of influences that determine traditional house forms.

House design is influenced through the

type and severity of climate. In climates that are not particularly severe the sheltering function of the house is reduced, and the local people may spend a large part of their day living out of doors. The type of climate – whether predominantly hot or cold, dry or wet – will influence the principal sheltering function of the house, such as whether its roof needs to keep off the rain or the sun or both. Usually, if rain is the more important factor, then roofs will be steeply sloped and overlapping the wall so as quickly to shed the water clear of the building; whereas in hot, dry climates a roof can be flat and put to other uses.

Ways of life

People who live nomadically usually want a light, transportable shelter that can be easily and quickly put up and taken down again, usually some form of tent. On the other hand, settled people such as farmers do not want to be continually building and rebuilding their houses; they want a permanent house that leaves them free to attend to their fields and in which to store food through the differing seasons.

Thus a people's way of life will influence the kind of house they build, although there will be diversity of house forms between people with essentially similar ways of life. Compare the yurt, the tepee and the Bedouin 'black tent'. These are three very different 'house' forms used by similar nomadic peoples. Within a fairly small area of Europe there are significant differences between peasant farmhouses in France, Switzerland and Italy, although the peasant way of life does not change much.

Technology

Tools, technical skills and technological knowledge can have both direct and indirect influences on house types and forms. The development of technology has been responsible for many changes in the design of people's houses, especially for those people who have been sufficiently wealthy or powerful to employ the work and skill of others. Indeed, except for the most primitive houses, the combined effects of wealth and of growing technical skills have probably led to the greatest differences in traditional houses. The most obvious developments have been in the making of bricks, of mortar, and of nails, pegs and ties of one kind or another. The development of metal tools, for instance, had a direct influence on the forms of timber frames that could be built, since they allowed precise shaping of the timbers and the use of strong rigid joints between frame members. Less directly, other technologies such as

transport have affected the choice of materials available to the house builder.

An assumption that it is easy (too easy) to make is that people will always choose the most 'advanced' form of technology available to them. Associated assumptions are that 'advanced' technology is more 'sophisticated' than 'primitive' forms and that technological 'progress' is a measure of 'civilization'. This assumption is not necessarily true; people develop and choose technologies for a variety of reasons, including social, economic, political and cultural reasons. There may be good social reasons, for example, why people prefer the village well to the more 'advanced' piping of water to individual houses. Perhaps drawing water from the well may be one of the few opportunities the local women have to meet one another. Or there may be symbolic values attached to particular forms of technology. An example in some new British houses of the past decade is the re-introduction of small-paned 'Georgian' windows instead of the more technologically 'advanced' large-paned picture window. Conversely, in some of the 'developing' countries traditional thatched roofs are replaced wherever possible with roofs of corrugated iron. The iron has higher status value because it is Western and 'advanced', and is used despite its very obvious drawbacks of being infernally hot in the sun and incredibly loud in the rain.

Economics

One of the major reasons for strong differences occurring between house designs in different societies is that there are often differing levels of economic development in those societies. A society that is materially rich has more wealth to devote to the construction of its artefacts than has a materially rather poor society. Industrialization and technological development have helped to generate wealth in modern societies that is spent, in part, on houses that are extraordinarily large, well-constructed, comfortable, well-appointed, etc. in comparison with the great majority of earlier houses.

Even within the same society there are often different economic 'classes' of people. Those who are richer can afford to purchase better materials, to employ skilled labour, to own larger pieces of land, and so on, all of which usually lead to their houses being significantly different to the houses of people in the poorer economic classes. In fact, differences in design that arise because of the greater wealth of the richer house owners are often deliberately emphasized in order to convey the owners' economic status.

13

Socio-cultural factors

Even where there are the severest limitations of materials, climate, technology, etc., people still find that they have *choice* available in their house forms. They can choose, for example, to build houses with one room or with many rooms; to lay out the house form in various symbolic patterns, or none at all; to build single-person, single-family or communal houses; to build their houses in isolation, or along 'streets', or around plazas. Perhaps the most severe climate and the most limited materials and technology are faced by the Eskimos, yet they *choose* to build three or four single-family igloos around a communal dance-hall.

It is in making these kinds of choice that socio-cultural factors will predominate in influencing the house design. For example, the layout of the house plan may be such as to reflect the relationships of various parts of the body, as is the case with the Dogon people (Figure 12), or the village plan may reflect the pattern of stars in the sky, as with the Pawnee Indians. A circular form for a house may be regarded as particularly propitious or holy, for example by the Hottentots and many others, or the house orientation may be determined by astrology, as in China. The division of spaces in the house may reflect division between the sexes, or marriage patterns, or kinship affiliations, or social hierarchies, or ritual functions...as happens everywhere in the world.

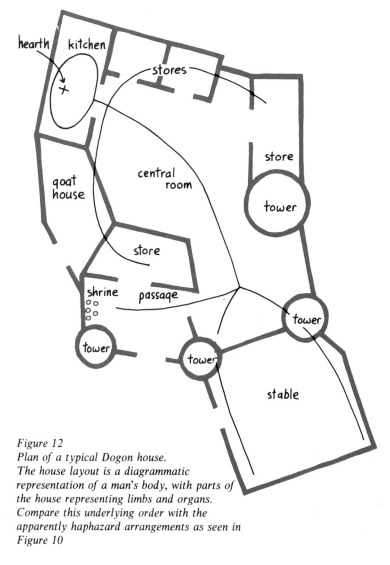

Figure 12
Plan of a typical Dogon house.
The house layout is a diagrammatic representation of a man's body, with parts of the house representing limbs and organs. Compare this underlying order with the apparently haphazard arrangements as seen in Figure 10

Before reading this section on 'Some reasons for diversity' you were asked to write your own notes suggesting some of the reasons. You have now read the author's own suggestions and analysis. He classifies the reasons under six headings:

materials,

climate,

ways of life,

technology,

economics,

socio-cultural factors.

Are these headings anything like your own? Look back at your own notes before reading on.

It doesn't matter whether you had something very similar to the author's headings. The important thing is that you should be comparing your thoughts with his, and helping yourself to learn what he is trying to teach by actively engaging your mind with the text.

Did you notice how the author organized his material for this section? He listed the reasons and then went on to discuss each of them in turn, with examples. When you come to write yourself (e.g. in assignments), remember these two virtues:

a clear, systematic layout, which helps the reader to grasp the structure of ideas, and

thus to understand them;

use of relevant examples, which help the reader to identify and remember the *general* point being made.

The author's six headings are not necessarily set out in any specific sequence or order; each type of reason is equally as important as any other. You could, therefore, have made your notes not in a 'linear' form (as the headings are set out above, line by line) but in a 'spray' form, like this:

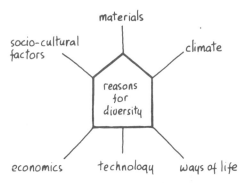

In this method you put the main subject (in this case, 'reasons for diversity') in the centre and arrange the various points around it. As you work on through the block you might like to try both 'linear' and 'spray' forms of note taking, to see which way best suits *you*.

3 To design a house

What should be clear by now is that diversity of house design (including Western peculiarities) arises from the diversity of human intentions and patterns of life within the limitations and possibilities of the material and financial resources available. To design a house, therefore, is to synthesize in quite a subtle way a great variety of factors; and the apparently 'simple' solution can be the most subtle when it is fully understood.

In attempting to summarize all the various factors in house design, I would suggest that there are two major categories: on the one hand the human requirements that make a house *necessary*, and on the other hand the technical capabilities that make a house *possible*. The human requirements include people's desires for convenience, comfort, symbolism, etc. in their houses. The technical capabilities include the materials, services, constructional techniques, etc. that people have at their disposal for building houses.

The relationship between these two major sets of factors, human requirements and technical capabilities, is by no means a simple one. It is not the case, for instance, that human beings simply decide what their requirements are and then use the available technology directly to meet those requirements. Instead, what people 'require' is usually heavily influenced by what they believe to be possible and what they can afford. Conversely, technology obviously does not exist and develop in a vacuum; people

suggest, demand and invent technical possibilities to meet their wants and needs.

Any one particular house, then, is one particular embodiment or expression of this relation between human requirements and technical capabilities at an acceptable cost. It 'sums up' the designer's attempt to synthesize these two major sets of factors in that particular design solution. So in order to design a house (or any other artefact) you need to know not only about human requirements and technical capabilities as though they were isolated one from another, but also how they interact in a design solution.

I have tried to convey this idea in a diagram (Figure 13) which sets out the study task facing you as a student. Figure 13 reads like this:

To design a house you need to know:

why people need a house,
how technology provides a house,
and some design skills.

People need a house because they have requirements such as:

physical comfort: their physiological needs for a warm, dry shelter;

domestic activities: their need for a convenient arrangement of spaces for activities such as preparing and eating meals, sleeping, talking, studying;

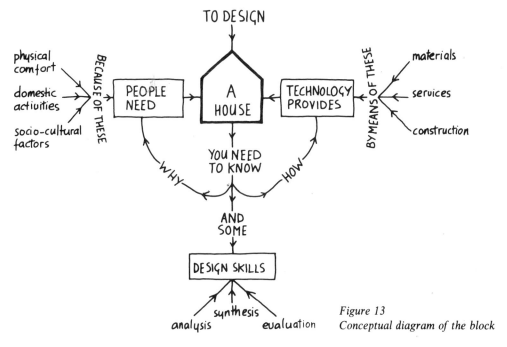

Figure 13
Conceptual diagram of the block

socio-cultural factors: their more intangible needs, which vary considerably between different cultures, such as their needs for privacy, personal identity, display.

Technology provides a house by means of:

materials: the extraction, processing and distribution of building materials of various kinds;

services: the provision of heat for warmth and cooking, water for drinking and washing, power for light and domestic tools, and the removal of wastes;

construction: the knowledge and techniques for constructing safe, sound, stable buildings.

The *design skills* you need are ones of:

analysis: the ability to investigate a design problem, to break it down into its component parts;

synthesis: the creative ability to generate design solutions, to build up again from the analysis;

evaluation: the ability to assess the suitability or measure the performance of a design solution.

Figure 13 summarizes all this and, I hope, presents it in a way that suggests that all the topics need to be integrated with each other, rather than considered in isolation. In Part Two you will be learning about many of these topics and how they interrelate in an actual house design. It is important to appreciate that many other factors and topics not included in Figure 13 will also influence a house design (not the least being the financial factor), but there is not enough time within this block to cover everything.

The last paragraph you have just read is one to pause over. When you are reading study material like this you need to be alert to any extra emphasis or statement about the structure of the argument. It is clear from this paragraph that this brief section 'To design a house' is very important. It relates to both Part One and Part Two of the block. In fact the diagram (Figure 13) reappears again later in the block. This repetition of the diagram, and its significant caption, *Conceptual diagram of the block*, suggest that it is a diagram that is worth 'reading' carefully.

Flick through until you find where the diagram appears for the second time.

It's in Section 11. Did you notice the two identical figures when you surveyed the block before starting to work on it?

Read the equally brief Section 11 'The story so far' that the diagram accompanies at the beginning of Part Three. It will help you to understand the whole structure of the block and its overall aims.

Don't be afraid, when studying, to skip about in this way, reading sections 'out of sequence'. You need to read flexibly,

sometimes changing the author's order (to suit your own purposes), or skimming (reading very quickly), or scanning (reading to spot key details). To plod through steadily can sometimes lead to boredom; lack of interest can produce lack of attention.

You probably found Part One relatively straightforward and easy to understand. It's important, though, to be able to express your understanding of key concepts in your own words. The following exercise helps you to do this.

Exercise

What is meant by the term 'socio-cultural' factors? Write a definition in your own words in the space below.

Discussion

It's by no means easy, is it? Your definition *might* look like one of the following:

People develop their own set of customs, habits and procedures in order to live together. The choices they make show their values as a society.

A society's values and traditions.

Intangible cultural influences.

Basically different ways of life according to different cultures, customs or traditions of different sets of people all over the world. It's reflected in the way they live together.

People are influenced by others in the groups in which they live. They prefer to continue to live in the manner to which they are accustomed, and which is accepted by those around them.

The term 'socio-cultural factors' (like many special terms) compresses a lot of meaning, and needs 'spelling out'. The third definition above clearly suffers from being too short, and says little more than the original term. The fourth definition also re-uses the word 'culture' without trying to define it. The first and last definitions are probably the best of the lot.

Part Two What is a house?

4 Introduction

Imagine yourself going to view a house that you are considering buying. You would try consciously to 'view' the house from different viewpoints. Are the rooms large enough? Are they conveniently planned? Does the structure look sound? Is the house easy to keep warm? Is there noise from neighbours? Can you afford it? And so on. You try quite deliberately to make yourself very critical towards the house, so that you won't overlook any of its potential shortcomings.

However, back in your own old house (or once you have bought the new one) you quickly let your level of critical awareness drop. You learn to live with the house's shortcomings because they are outweighed by its advantages, or you adjust your patterns of living so as to manage within the house as it is, not as it ideally might be. Few of us ever manage to find, or to afford, our ideal dream house.

In Part Two of this block my aim is to help you to develop your critical awareness of a house from many different viewpoints. This is not simply to help you if you are buying a new house. Rather, it is to try to develop in you an awareness of a house as a designed artefact. I shall be trying to get you to develop a designer's view of a house, and this is a view that sees the house simultaneously in many separate ways and also *as a whole*, because the designer of any artefact sees his design as a combination, or synthesis, of many separate factors.

What better example of a house could I choose on which to base my teaching than your own house? Throughout this part of the block you will be asked to carry out study activities that are based on your own house. The purpose of these activities is not only to reinforce your learning from the text by applying the theoretical knowledge to a practical example, but also to provide you with practice in the design skills of analysing and evaluating. You will learn how to 'model' your house from different viewpoints and in ways that encourage and enable you to 'see' it more clearly from these various viewpoints.

Obviously, I am assuming that you do, in fact, have a house of your own that you can use as the example in the activities. In some cases, the activities also assume that this house is a fairly conventional one: terraced, detached or semi-detached; probably two-storeyed, and so on. If you don't live in such a conventional house, then I'm afraid some of the activities will be impossible or irrelevant for you. The relevance of the activities will depend on what kind of 'house' you actually live in. If it's a family-sized flat, then most of them will still be relevant, but if it's only a small bed-sitter, then most of them probably won't be. If you find that you are stuck in this way, then you might consider using as your example someone else's house that you know well, such as your parents' or that of a friend.

In all the activities you will see that I have carried out the instructions myself, using my own house as the example, so that you can see exactly what the instructions mean, and what you have to do.

Exercise

What do you think was the purpose of the 'Introduction' you have just read? Look back over it and underline one sentence that seems to you to convey the purpose of the 'Introduction' most clearly. Write down in your own words what you think the purpose of the 'Introduction' was.

Discussion

The purposes of the 'Introduction' seem to have been to convey the author's main aims for Part Two of the block, and to give you some idea of what you will be doing in working through it. The first sentence of the third paragraph is a clear statement of an aim. You may have underlined another sentence, but check back to satisfy yourself that the sentence you chose does clearly convey something of the author's purposes in writing an introduction. The third and fourth paragraphs seem to be the most important in conveying these purposes.

In a previous study note you were asked to notice how the author had organized his material. Introductions and conclusions are particularly significant (or, at least, they *should* be) and need close attention. Don't forget this yourself when you come to write *your own* essay assignments later in the course.

Figure 14   Children's drawings of houses

5 Home and culture

If you ask a child to draw a picture of a house, you know quite well what the resulting picture will be like, much like those in Figure 14. The result is not surprising; in fact it is extraordinarily predictable: the child draws something that closely resembles the symbol of 'house' in Western culture. What is perhaps surprising is that most children in Western cultures draw very similar pictures of 'a house' from quite early ages and regardless of what kind of house they actually live in themselves. Children who live in blocks of flats, or in terraced houses, in bungalows or in caravans, still tend to draw a picture of a detached, two-storey, pitched-roof house.

Clearly, the children must pick up this symbol of 'house' from sources other than their own direct experience of real houses; from their picture books, say, or from the pictures adults draw for them of 'a house'. Perhaps if you asked a child to draw a picture of his or her *own* house, the result might be different from the conventional symbol of 'a house'.

The fact that quite young children have already absorbed the symbol of 'house' that predominates in their culture is an indication of how strong but subtle is the imposition of cultural norms. These cultural norms, or standards, or expectations, can therefore have an important influence in design, even though they might never be made explicit. In some cases, cultural factors have led to the development or adoption of house designs that are functionally quite unsuited to their physical locality. I have already mentioned how in some 'Third-World' countries there is such high status associated with Western materials that corrugated iron is used for roofing even though it creates a very uncomfortable shelter.

A clear example of this cultural 'colonization by design' is provided by the spread throughout Japan of what is now regarded as the traditional Japanese house design. This design is based on the use of a very light timber frame, with quite flimsy sliding screen-walls that allow the house to be opened up completely. The roof, with its overhangs and distinctive shapes, is the most important feature of the house, both functionally and symbolically. This kind of design, with a heavy roof to keep off rain but with open sides to allow air to circulate, is usually associated with a hot, humid climate. (The relationship between climate and design is discussed in Section 8.) And the Japanese design in fact originated in the southernmost

island of Japan, Kyushu, where the climate is indeed sub-tropical. However, as the people of this region gradually colonized and spread northwards through the Japanese islands, they took their house design with them and it was even adopted by the people living in the northernmost islands despite the fact that the climate there is predominantly cold. The design from the southern islands is quite unsuited, climatically, to the northern islands.

Other clear examples of the dominance of cultural factors in house forms arise where culturally distinct groups of people inhabit similar or even identical regions but develop different house forms. One such example is provided by the different house forms of the Pueblo and Navajo Indians, who both inhabit the semi-desert region of south-western North America.

As you saw in Section 1, the Pueblo Indians build a rather 'urban' form of compact, terraced, multi-storey housing, built in an *ad hoc* additive style around an open plaza or along broad streets. As well as the streets and plaza, the flat roofs are all communal territory and a general community-oriented attitude prevails in Pueblo culture, reflected in their communal architecture.

The Navajo Indians, in contrast, build detached houses, called hogans, consisting of mud walls around a log frame. Several hogans will usually be built close together, housing related families, but each family has its own hogan.

However, each hogan is more than a simple house, it is also a sacred place and its enclosed space is psychologically as well as physically quite distinct from the world of the 'outside'. Many features of the hogan – its basic forms, its internal arrangement, the orientation of the door, etc. – are enshrined in Navajo mythology and are important in various rituals. Thus there is great resistance to any change in its design. In his article 'The pueblo and the hogan' (in P. Oliver, ed., *Shelter and Society*, Barrie & Jenkins, 1969, pp. 66–79) Amos Rapoport comments as follows on the differences between the pueblo and the hogan:

‘Both the hogan and the pueblo occupy the same physical environment. They are built by people with a similar economic and technological base, who have been in contact for hundreds of years and have profoundly influenced each other and who have both been affected by Spanish and American contact. It would, therefore, appear that the key to the great differences in the built forms is *choice* – and that this choice depends on what people regard as important, that is, on the world view expressed in social organization, religion and ritual.

The purpose of Navajo ritual is basically to restore harmony within the individual and between the individual and other people or supernatural forces. The basic theme of almost all Pueblo ritual, on the other hand, is to restore harmony in the whole universe. Navajo language leads to sharply defined categories, the filing away of things in tight little categories and tends to lead to differences rather than similarities being noticed. The Pueblo Indians stress the continuity of life and death, the relationship between the living and the dead, whereas the Navajo fear and abhor death and the dead.

All these differences in world view help to account not only for many specifics of life and culture but the different forms of dwelling. In this light we can better understand the pueblo, which is *always* a basically communal building housing a group, while the hogan, although often grouped, is basically an individual family dwelling and may be on its own.' (pp. 77–8.)

Figure 15   Plaza-type pueblo town, Taos, New Mexico, USA

Figure 16   Plans of (a) street-type and (b) plaza-type pueblo towns

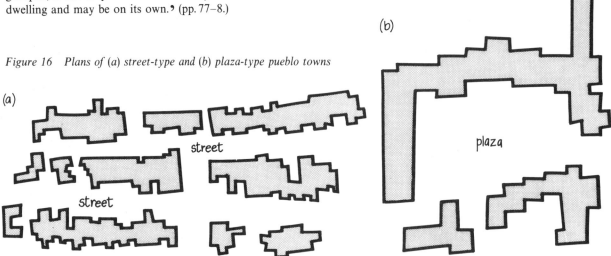

(b)

(a)

street

street

plaza

Figure 17
Typical section through a pueblo terrace

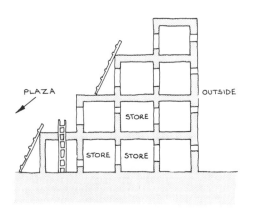

PLAZA

OUTSIDE

STORE

STORE   STORE

Figure 18   'Cutaway' view of a pueblo house

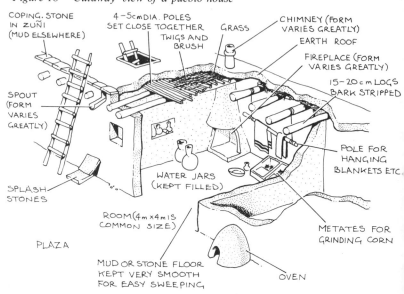

COPING. STONE IN ZUÑI (MUD ELSEWHERE)

4–5cmDIA. POLES SET CLOSE TOGETHER TWIGS AND BRUSH

GRASS

CHIMNEY (FORM VARIES GREATLY)

EARTH ROOF

FIREPLACE (FORM VARIES GREATLY)

15–20 cm LOGS BARK STRIPPED

SPOUT (FORM VARIES GREATLY)

POLE FOR HANGING BLANKETS ETC.

SPLASH STONES

WATER JARS (KEPT FILLED)

ROOM (4m x 4m IS COMMON SIZE)

PLAZA

MUD OR STONE FLOOR KEPT VERY SMOOTH FOR EASY SWEEPING

OVEN

METATES FOR GRINDING CORN

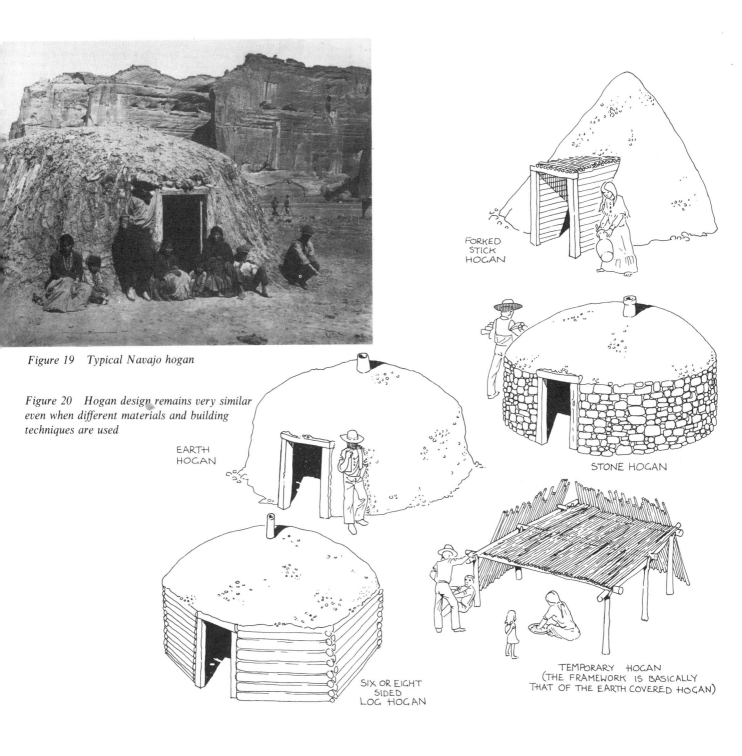

Figure 19   Typical Navajo hogan

Figure 20   Hogan design remains very similar even when different materials and building techniques are used

FORKED STICK HOGAN

STONE HOGAN

EARTH HOGAN

SIX OR EIGHT SIDED LOG HOGAN

TEMPORARY HOGAN (THE FRAMEWORK IS BASICALLY THAT OF THE EARTH COVERED HOGAN)

Figure 21   Construction method for earth-covered hogan (all others are similar)

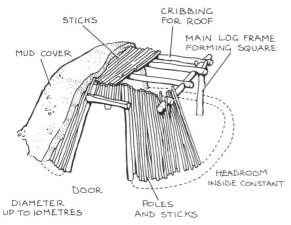

STICKS

CRIBBING FOR ROOF

MUD COVER

MAIN LOG FRAME FORMING SQUARE

HEADROOM INSIDE CONSTANT

DOOR

DIAMETER UP TO 10 METRES

POLES AND STICKS

Figure 22   Diagrammatic plan of the standard internal layout of all hogans

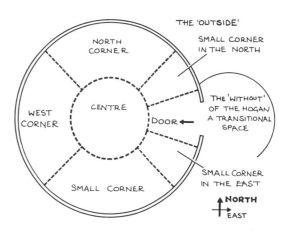

THE 'OUTSIDE'

NORTH CORNER

SMALL CORNER IN THE NORTH

WEST CORNER

CENTRE

THE 'WITHOUT' OF THE HOGAN A TRANSITIONAL SPACE

DOOR

SMALL CORNER

SMALL CORNER IN THE EAST

NORTH
EAST

21

In contrast to the continuity of design and resistance to change that is usually present in traditional cultures, house design in the West has been subject in this century to what might now seem to be extraordinary degrees of experimentation. There have been changes not only in internal arrangements of rooms and so on, but also radical changes in external appearances as new materials, new constructional techniques and new architectural ideas have been tried. Despite the common stereotypes in children's house drawings, it is perhaps difficult for Westerners to agree collectively on what is 'a house'.

A striking example of architectural experimentation apparently going too far is provided by the houses built at Pessac, near Bordeaux, France, in the 1920s, which were designed by the influential Franco-Swiss architect known as Le Corbusier. There is an estate of about fifty houses, some detached, some semi-detached and some in terraces. Le Corbusier was given a free architectural rein by his client, M Henri Frugès, and from its inception the project was regarded as something of an experiment. The houses were generally of a very simple, but radical, internal plan, and also incorporated novel features such as flat roofs with terraces or roof gardens. Externally, the houses were equally simple, 'cubist' forms, notable for their plain concrete surfaces and wide windows (Figure 23). As a concession to his client Le Corbusier allowed the plain external wall surfaces to be painted in a limited variety of muted colours. (One of the children's drawings in Figure 14 is by a six-year-old girl who had only lived in a Pessac house. Can you identify which one?*)

The reaction of local people to this estate was quick and to the point: it became known as 'the Arab quarter' or 'the Moroccan

Figure 23   Le Corbusier's houses at Pessac: before (1926)...

Figure 24   ...and after (1966)

Figure 25   Adaptations (left) to another of the original house types (below) at Pessac: the mid-flight landing of the open, external staircase has been covered to form a balcony, the open area beneath the staircase has been enclosed, the wide windows have survived, but the wall surfaces have been given a different treatment

* It is the one at the top left. The windows in that drawing are perhaps significantly wider and more 'Corbusian' than in any of the other drawings.

district'. The architecture reminded them not of their conventional symbols for 'house', but of symbols (e.g. flat roofs, plain surfaces) from the traditional houses they would have seen (or seen pictures of) in the French colonies of North Africa.

What is more interesting now, perhaps, is not so much the original design but the striking changes that have been made to the houses over the intervening sixty years by their occupants.

Some of the houses (Figures 24 and 25) are quite unrecognizable as 'Corbusian' designs: the wide windows have been narrowed to more conventional dimensions, and sometimes reshaped altogether; ground-floor patios and roof terraces have been enclosed to create extra rooms; external staircase landings have become balcony loggias; the flat roofs have been pedimented; various signs of 'personalization' by the owner–occupants abound.

The desire to 'personalize' one's house, is not, though, confined to examples of radical modern design. It occurs even in fairly conventional houses, where colours and added facing materials often change from one house to the next as people adapt their standard 'semi' into something more individualistic.

The lessons from 'experiments' such as the Pessac housing are slowly being learnt by architects; notably the lesson that 'a house' usually conveys more symbolic meanings to people than can be represented by a rationalized cube. Some architects have now turned fairly deliberately to the inclusion of more symbolic elements in their designs (Figure 26). The potential danger of this approach is the adoption and development of functionally inadequate designs simply because they are in some way 'symbolic', just as in the north of Japan people shivered in the flimsy southern-style houses because that style was symbolic of 'advanced' culture.

Exercise

In your notebook, make some notes on what seem to be the main points in the 'Home and culture' section. Don't write more than five or six points and don't take more than about fifteen minutes over it. You can look back at the section, but first try to see how many points you can write down from memory.

Discussion

Your notes may look something like this:

'Cultural norms' (remember to define in your own words, e.g. 'the standards accepted by a society or group') are important influences on house design.

In the West there has been much experiment in house design.

People like to 'personalize' their houses, and architects need to remember this.

Now read the author's own summary overleaf. Compare it with the notes above and with your own notes. Are there differences?

Probably there are. Notes are personal things: you take as many or as few as *you* need, to recall or summarize the main points. So don't worry about differences between your notes and those printed here.

An important note-taking skill is to be able to recognize the difference between:

the statement of a main point, idea or concept;

examples of the point.

If you look back over the section with this in

Figure 26 (a) *This modern American house (architects: Venturi and Rauch, 1975) has a symbolically emphasized roof, which, whether by design or by accident, has a striking similarity with the roof of (b) the traditional Swiss farmhouse (architects: anonymous). There is, however, a pedigree of evolutionary design in the Swiss farmhouse that is both symbolic and functional*

(a)

(b)

mind, you will see that the structure of the argument might be represented like this:

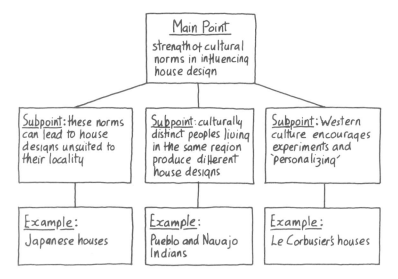

This is a 'tree' diagram (it's like the branches of a tree, upside down). If you compare it with 'linear' or 'spray' forms of notes, you can see that it's somewhere between the two. It is a useful form for setting out the structure of an argument that has main points, subpoints and so on.

Exercise

You might have noticed that a good deal of the 'Home and culture' section was devoted to examples. Why do you think the author chose to use so many examples?

Summary

In this section you have learnt that there is a strong cultural influence on the design of houses, sometimes producing house designs that are not well-suited to their objective requirements such as providing adequate shelter from the climate. Even where houses adequately meet the same objective requirements (such as those of the Pueblo and Navajo Indians) they can be radically different in design, due to different cultural influences. The symbolically ideal house in our own culture tends to be single-family, detached, two-storeyed, pitch-roofed. People also often like to personalize the appearance of their house.

Discussion

Examples help readers to group the main ideas. They add life and substance to the text, and help readers to relate the ideas and theories to their own experiences. Often, the ideas are themselves derived by generalizing from many examples.

Activity 1   Your own house's face

The purpose of this activity is to begin a design analysis of your own house, starting from the outside (the 'face' your house presents to you and your neighbours) and, in later activities, working inwards to the plan and other details. (Estimated activity time: about ½–1 hour.)

1   From memory (i.e. do it straight away, without first going outside to look) draw the front of your house. Don't worry about details that you cannot remember, but try to make your drawing as clear and as detailed as you can, although obviously you probably won't be skilled at drawing and your attempt may in fact be fairly 'childish'. Try asking other members of your household to make their own drawings, too, without looking at each other's until you have all finished. (As with all these activities, my own attempt is shown alongside.)

My drawing of the front of our house, from memory

2   Compare your drawings one with another. Are there any large differences between what you each remember and have drawn? Has someone in the family clearly got a better memory of all the details of the front of your house, or do you disagree among yourselves as to the details and their relative locations?

My daughter's drawing of the front of our house, from memory

3   Now go and look at the front of your house and compare the reality with the drawings. Are there any large differences between the reality and what is supposed to be represented on the drawings? Did you have a good visual memory of the front of your house, or have you not really looked carefully at it before? Try making another drawing from observation, to improve on your first attempt.

A photograph of my house (the one in the middle)

6 House and self

Before reading this section read the summary at the end. Try rapidly skim-reading the section to identify the points made in the summary. When you skim you move very quickly over the words, trying to spot the main points and to distinguish these from examples or other amplification. You will often find the main ideas at the beginnings or ends of paragraphs. Your purpose in skimming is to locate these main points and to uncover the structure of the argument. You will find that a good deal of this section is again taken up with examples.

As always, you should adapt the skimming method to suit yourself. For example, it is suggested above that you should look for the main ideas. But if you are the kind of person who learns best from concrete details, then it may be better for you to look for the examples first, and then to move from these to the general ideas that they illustrate. Experiment and see which suits you; always feel free to adapt any of the advice given in these study notes to suit your own way of working and learning.

'We shape our houses; and our houses shape us,' said Churchill. He meant that there is an important psychological relationship between our things and our selves, referring particularly to the things we live with, and in, every day: our houses. In a sense, we are 'shaped' as individuals by the shape of our environment, whether it is natural or human-made. You have seen this relation already in some of the interactions between 'simple' shelters and their builder–occupants. Particularly where there are strong connections between house form and a people's mythology, religion or rituals, the house form continually reinforces both collective and individual patterns of behaviour and cultural beliefs. The contrasting examples of the pueblo and the hogan, for instance, show that not only does house form reflect a people's social attitudes and cultural codes, but also that it helps to determine, and to inhibit change in, those attitudes and codes.

It is perhaps easy to overplay the importance and to overemphasize the influence of the physical, human-made environment on individual behaviour and attitudes; although environmental psychologists have naturally tended to emphasize the fact that the environment has *some* influence on people. The psychological importance of the environment is perhaps most clearly and frighteningly demonstrated by some of the inhumane modern torture techniques in which a person is placed in a situation that is essentially an environmental blank, in which there is nothing to see, touch or hear. The result of this deprivation of environmental stimulus is usually a fairly rapid psychological breakdown.

On the other hand, you would rightly be sceptical of any claim that the physical environment was *the* major determinant of your behaviour and personality; social, cultural and personal factors are surely more important. Yet details of the environment certainly do *influence* your behaviour, even though they may not *determine* it: you cannot pass through a wall unless there is an opening in it, but you may choose whether or not to use the opening; you cannot see out of a room unless a window is provided, but you can choose whether or not to look out. In many cases it is the planners and designers who are thwarted in their attempts to determine people's behaviour through the design of the environment. People perversely (or so it seems to the planners) choose the 'wrong' routes, ignore signs, climb over barriers, adapt things to uses they were never designed for, and so on.

Again, Le Corbusier's houses at Pessac provide an interesting example. In addition to the changes in external appearance I have already mentioned, the owner–occupiers of these houses have made many changes to the internal room arrangements. Figure 27(b) shows some of the rearrangements that have been made in the simple three-room ground-floor plan of the most common house type at Pessac. The internal and external changes made to the Pessac houses are often so very different from the original designs (Figure 27a), that one's first thought must be that the architect's 'experiment' was a complete failure, the designs simply were not what people wanted. Indeed, Le Corbusier himself said, speaking of the Pessac houses, 'it is always life that is right and the architect who is wrong'.

However, it must be said in defence of the original designs that they did at least (whether intentionally or unintentionally) *allow* the occupants to make radical changes to suit themselves. The simple plans, for example, allow and perhaps even encourage a wide variety of alterations. The provision of covered and partly enclosed external spaces makes extensions and additions of internal spaces a good deal easier than is usually the case. The wide windows can easily be filled in, while the converse (extending small windows) is not at all easy. The odd, undefined room (the 'parlour') included in the original plan is used for a variety of purposes: as an entrance

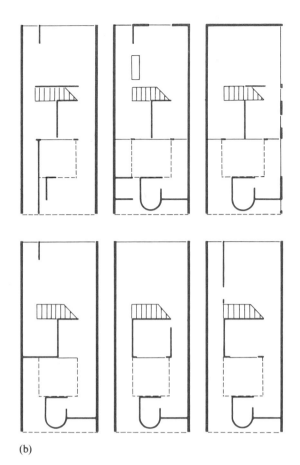

Figure 27 (a) *The original ground-floor and first-floor plans of the terraced house-type at Pessac;*

(b) *some of the many ground-floor plan changes made by owners of this house-type*

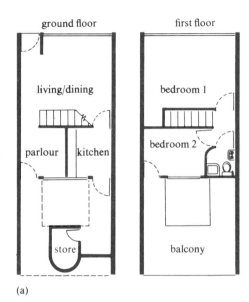

(a)

(b)

hall, study, bedroom, 'rest-room', and even as a hairdressing salon – these are all uses decided by the occupants, not by the architect. Even the plain exterior wall surfaces lend themselves easily to personalized decoration. As one of the owner–occupiers said, 'I bought this house in five minutes flat; I didn't like the outside at all, but I saw its potential at once...it's the sort of house where you could introduce all manner of combinations.'

The interior plan of a house can have a real influence on the life-style that is possible within it. The way in which the owners of the Pessac houses adapted their house interiors suggests that, even within a fairly small group of basically similar families, people feel the need to adapt their house plan to their particular preferences. The original design of a house can be very critical in terms of how much re-design it allows without major (i.e. expensive) alterations. Even the number of different furniture arrangements can be severely limited by the placing of walls, doors and windows.

Figure 28 shows the furniture arrangements that were found in use in different apartments in a block of flats in Sweden. This particular block of flats was of an experimental design with demountable internal walls for each apartment, so that the interior room arrangements could be altered quite easily by the occupants, to suit themselves. In Figure 28 none of the internal walls are shown, just the occupants' furniture arrangements. Even so, the wall locations are not difficult to identify, and there is considerable conformity

in furniture arrangements; only one or two 'deviants' have used 'unusual' locations for their beds, for instance. The influence of window positions is particularly noticeable.

Strong criticisms of conventional Western house designs and particularly of their implications for personal and family life-styles have emerged from the women's movement. Ideas such as 'a woman's place is in the home' and of housework being a 'woman's work', which is also 'never done', are quite strongly embedded in Western culture. These ideas are unconsciously reflected in many aspects of conventional house design that therefore reinforce the conventional role of the woman in her house and household. The kitchen, in particular, is regarded as the woman's domain and the kitchen, in a sense, completely captures the woman. Imagine, if you can, a kitchenless house and imagine the implications of such a house for the conventional woman's role; there is virtually no 'place' for such a woman in such a house.

If the house is an important influence on people's life-styles and on the way people see themselves, it is surprising that so few people live in houses they have designed for themselves. In fact, almost everyone has to rely on the products of the housing industry, rather than housing themselves, just as they have to rely on the products and services of all the other industries of an industrial society. This means that people live in houses designed by someone else for someone else, for anonymous, average, mass-standard 'persons'. Individualistic houses are almost non-existent in Britain and Western Europe.

27

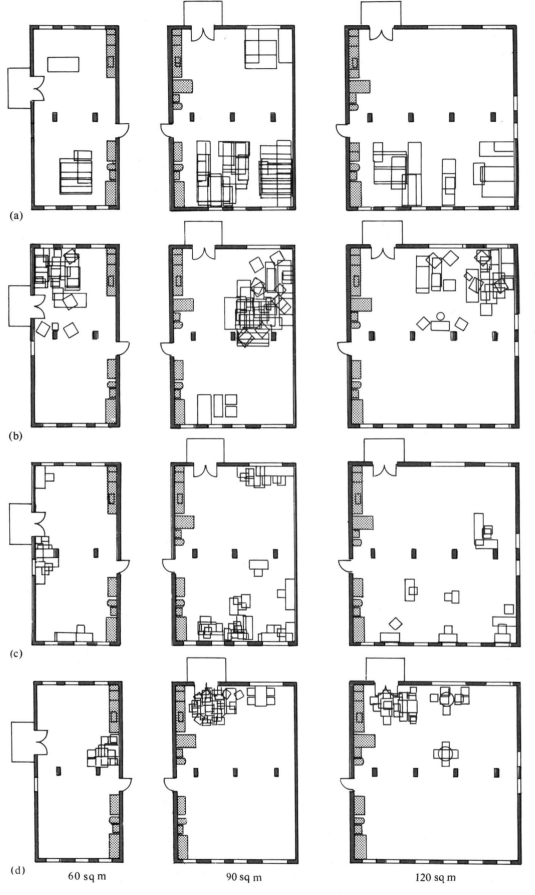

Figure 28 The various furniture arrangements that were found to be in use in a block of Swedish flats. The flats have internal walls that can be rearranged; the only fixtures are a few structural columns and the plumbing installations (shown shaded). There are three sizes of flat: 60 m², 90 m² and 120 m². The plans show: (a) the bed locations that were found to be in use; (b) the locations of living-room furniture; (c) the study desk locations; and (d) the dining furniture locations. In each plan, the furniture locations found in all the similar flats in the block are all superimposed. Notice how, despite the apparent freedom of the occupants to rearrange their flats, there is considerable conformity in the locations that were chosen for the furniture and therefore in the use of the plans

(a)

(b)

(c)

(d)

60 sq m   90 sq m   120 sq m

Most people live in 'housing' rather than their own house: in housing estates, housing developments, housing blocks, etc.

This is symptomatic of living in an industrialized society. One of the costs to be borne in return for the benefits of industrialization has been a gradual fragmentation and specialization of work-roles. In traditional societies someone can be the owner–occupant–builder–designer of his or her own house, but these various roles are separated and specialized in industrial societies (Figure 29).

Of course, even in industrial societies it is *possible* for individuals still to synthesize all the roles and provide themselves with their own house. When this happens it is often the work of an idiosyncratic personality, and the resulting design is usually equally idiosyncratic, as in the examples from North America shown in Figures 30–3. Nearer home, it is still possible for a Frenchman's house to become his castle and for an Englishman's house to become his nostalgic railway station (Figures 34 and 35).

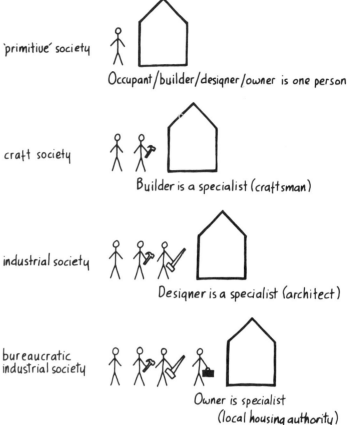

'primitive' society
Occupant/builder/designer/owner is one person

craft society
Builder is a specialist (craftsman)

industrial society
Designer is a specialist (architect)

bureaucratic industrial society
Owner is specialist (local housing authority)

Figure 29
The fragmentation of roles as society becomes more industrialized

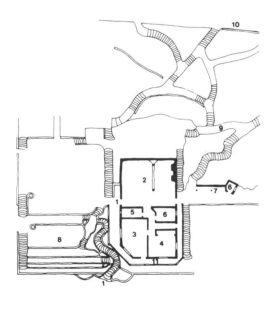

Figure 30   Art Beal's house, West Cambria Pines, California, USA. Key: 1 entrance, 2 living room, 3 kitchen, 4 bedroom, 5 storage, 6 bathroom, 7 workshop, 8 terrace garden, 9 steps, 10 storage shed, 11 porch

Figure 31 Fred Burn's house, Belfast, Maine,
USA. Key: 1 entrance, 2 kitchen/living room,
3 bedroom, 4 storage, 5 bathroom, 6 shed

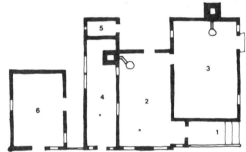

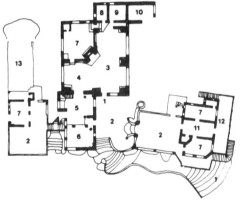

Figure 32 Boyce Luther Gulley's house,
Phoenix, Arizona, USA. Key: 1 entrance,
2 terrace, 3 living room, 4 dining room,
5 kitchen, 6 breakfast room, 7 bedroom,
8 bathroom, 9 dressing room, 10 storage, 11 hall,
12 porch, 13 pool

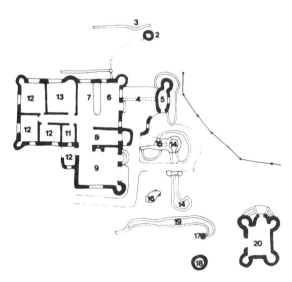

Figure 33   George Plumb's house, Duncan, British Columbia, Canada. Key: *1 entrance, 2 coke bottle, 3 bottle wall, 4 welcome sign, 5 wall, 6 kitchen, 7 dining room, 8 storage, 9 shop/museum, 10 porch, 11 bathroom, 12 bedroom, 13 den, 14 fish pond, 15 waterfall, 16 elephant, 17 totem pole, 18 Leaning Tower of Pisa, 19 lily pond, 20 studio*

Figure 34   A Frenchman's home is his castle: a bungalow with additions at Berck-sur-Plage

Figure 35   An Englishman's home is his railway station: nostalgic topiary at Rangeworthy, Gloucestershire

Summary

This section has introduced the idea that the plan of a house can have some influence on the kind of life-style that is possible within that plan. In cultures with very strong traditions related to house forms the plan is usually a reflection or embodiment of those traditions. In Western culture such traditions are not so strong and there is consequently less restraint on the details of family life-style. This is reflected in the fact that people often want to adapt or modify 'standard' house plans better to suit themselves. It is not always possible to make such modifications and, in particular, it is rare to find houses that are designed individualistically.

This block is divided into separate sections, but it is important to see how these relate to each other.

Exercise

Look back over the last two sections and at their summaries. Can you identify one key theme that runs through both sections?

Discussion

Both sections discuss the importance of cultural influences on house design. The overall design (including shape, appearance and plan) is influenced in important ways by the values and priorities of the people who designed it.

Activity 2 Your house plan

The purpose of this activity is to help you to make a reasonably accurate plan of your house, which you will need for later activities. (Estimated activity time: about 1–2 hours.)

1 Draw from memory the plan of your house (all the plans if it has two or more floors). As with the previous activity it is not important to get all the details right at your first attempt, and again it may be interesting to get other members of your household to try doing the same. Include what details of the building you can remember, such as door and window positions, but do not worry about including furniture. Try to draw it to scale, that is, taking care about the shapes of the rooms, and their sizes and positions relative to one another.

2 Now use your drawing as a guide (as a 'map') to your house, to check how accurate the drawing is. Walk slowly through your house (starting, say, at the front door) with your plan in your hand, and imagine yourself also 'in' the drawing, suitably scaled-down to size. Check on the accuracy of the drawing relative to the real house by noting the positions of doors and windows, counting paces between doors, and so on.

These simultaneous real and imaginary walks through the real plan and its drawn representation should not only help you to check the accuracy of the drawing but also help you to understand how to read a plan drawing.

3 If it is necessary (because your first attempt contained major errors), re-draw the plan so that it is a reasonable reflection of reality. Try to think of the reasons why you made any mistakes in the first drawing. Had you simply forgotten some

My rough sketch plans of my house, from memory

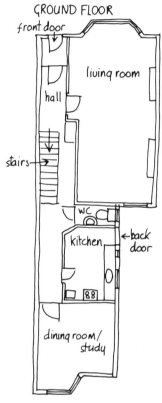

My daughter's sketch plans of our house, from memory

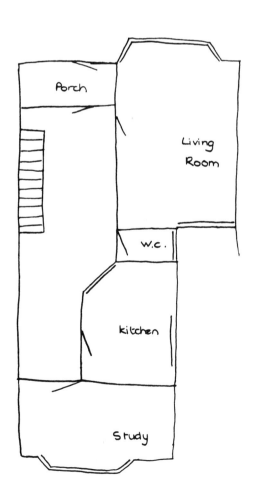

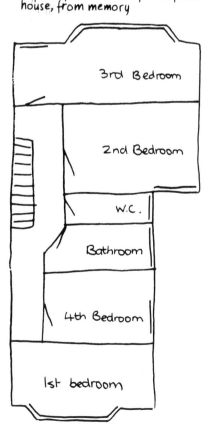

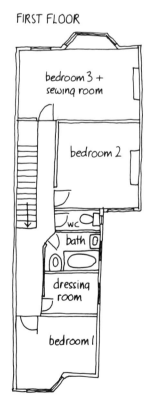

of the details, or were you not aware of them? Did you get some of the sizes and shapes wrong; perhaps the house (or some parts of it) 'felt' smaller or larger in your memory than it is in reality? Were there any significant differences between the plans drawn by different people? Do these differences perhaps reflect different 'perceptions' or mental images of the house?

4   Write the 'names' describing your use of the various rooms ('living room' etc.) on the drawing. Think about the assumptions that underlie this 'naming of parts'. Why is the house divided into these particular special uses? Think also about the assumptions that underlie the original plan. Did you have much choice in allocating different uses to different rooms when you moved into the house, or were you practically forced to use the house in the way its designer assumed you would?

5   You will need reasonably accurate plans of your house for the remaining activities in Part Two. It may be that you have found that you can already make quite an accurate scale plan (i.e. the rooms are all the right shapes and sizes relative to each other, and the doors and windows are the right sizes and in the right places). But if not, re-draw (and *keep* re-drawing) your plans until you are confident that they are a good representation of reality. You should aim to get your plans about as good as my own rough sketch plans of my house, which you can compare with 'reality' by checking my sketches with the accurately drawn scale plans I have provided just for this purpose.

To check the accuracy of your plans I suggest that you re-draw (as separate, trial drawings) at least two or three of the rooms *to scale*. That is, measure with a tape-measure the dimensions of the actual room and the positions of doors, windows, etc., and then with a ruler draw out the plan so that all the dimensions are accurately reduced to the same scale. A useful scale reduction to use is 1:100; that means that every dimension on the scale plan is exactly one-hundredth of the dimension it represents in the real house. So a room of, say, 3.5 metres (i.e. 3 metres, 50 centimetres) by 4.2 metres (i.e. 4 m, 20 cm) would be drawn as 3.5 centimetres by 4.2 centimetres at 1:100 scale. If you used squared paper of 1 cm × 1 cm squares, it will help make the scaling easier.

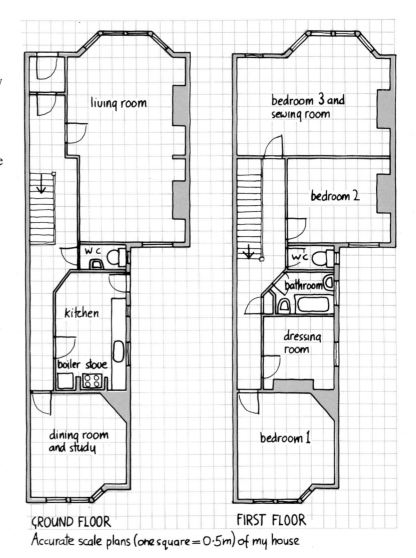

GROUND FLOOR   FIRST FLOOR

Accurate scale plans (one square = 0.5m) of my house

7 Planning for convenience

You should by now be practising some of the study skills recommended earlier. So, before reading this section, decide how you intend to tackle it. Before proceeding to read it carefully you might:

skim-read it,

read the summary of the section *first*,

write down for yourself what you think will be covered and compare your notes with what the author chooses to say.

Earlier study notes have given you practice in these techniques. Choose your own way of 'getting into' the section and of studying it actively.

One of the most important aspects of a house is that the arrangement of its rooms should be suited to and convenient for the people who live in it. I mean that there should be enough separate rooms big enough to cater for the occupants' separate activities, and the rooms should be placed one-to-another in a convenient way (e.g. the kitchen next to the dining room). In the design of a house with several rooms there are inevitably some problems connected with the relationships of the rooms to one another. For instance, which rooms should be next to each other or, conversely, placed as far apart as possible? Which rooms should have interconnecting doors? Given a particular arrangement of rooms in a plan, which ones could best be used for what purposes? And so on.

While reading the last section you probably began to think about some of these questions in respect of your own house. In fact, in your own house you must have already answered some of the questions, when you decided which rooms were to be used for what; although there might not have been much choice for you.

In this section I shall be discussing in general terms the questions of room planning within houses. I want you to develop an aware, and perhaps critical, view of the influences that affect the interior planning of houses, so that you no longer necessarily take for granted the conventional arrangement of rooms in a house plan, or the arrangement of furniture etc. within a room. This critical awareness should begin to lead you into considerations of how plans *might* be arranged.

As you have already seen, there are not only *functional* but also *cultural* factors that influence house design. The functional factors

are ones for which an objective or rational explanation can be given for the plan arrangement, such as putting the main living room on the warm, south side in a cool northern climate. The cultural factors arise from the social habits and customs of the people who have developed a particular arrangement of their house plan, such as having the house entrance always facing east for religious reasons.

In Western society it is sometimes difficult to separate 'functional' and 'cultural' factors because the cultural norms are often rationality, efficiency and 'function' itself. That is to say, people in Western society prefer a house plan that is functional and efficient in its interior planning because they have come to believe that this is the best way to plan a house, rather than to use religious or other symbolic reasoning.

This is not the case in most other cultures, where factors such as customs, religious observances and ceremonial events may have explicit influences on the interior planning of a house. One of the most complex set of rules for house interiors occurs in traditional house design in Madagascar, where the house has to contain twelve internal divisions.

'Each division has a different use, such as rice or water jar storage, according to religious prescriptions which also affect the furniture arrangement; the bed, for example, is always in the east, with its head to the north. The main facade with the door and windows faces west, since west is the principal direction, the people call themselves "those who face the West", and the house is closely related to the religious plan of the universe. The north is the entry for notable visitors, the northeast corner is the most sacred, and the north wall is the place for the ancestor cult. If someone is to be honored he is invited to take the north place.' (Amos Rapoport, *House Form and Culture*, Prentice-Hall, 1969, p. 55.)

Even in houses with a single room there are often fixed, traditional arrangements of furniture, household objects and seating positions. Figure 36 shows the traditional interior plan of a Mongol yurt. It is subdivided (by conventions, not by any physical divisions) into a men's side and a women's side, and there is a social hierarchy of sitting positions. Subdividing a house into men's and women's areas is a common

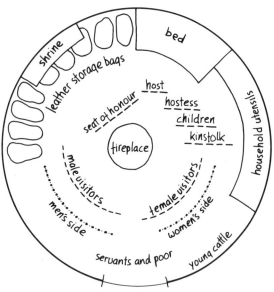

Figure 36   The conventional interior plan arrangement of a Mongol yurt

feature in many cultures, including, as I suggested earlier, Western culture, where the kitchen is often regarded as a woman's domain.

Can you think of other traditions and customs in British culture that have similar relevance in the design of houses?

There are many customs, such as into which rooms visitors and strangers may be invited, whether friends, neighbours, tradespeople, etc. should use the 'front' or 'back' door, keeping a parlour for 'best' use. Some families also have particular customs of their own, such as which chair (and its location) 'belongs' to whom.

It is common for there also to be subcultural differences in the way people use their homes. That is, within a culture there are subgroups who have different conventions, standards, values, etc. In Western culture, for example, there are subcultural differences between the various socio-economic classes: conventions in a working-class home often differ from those in a middle-class home.

Some of these differences have rather accidentally emerged in the design of houses for working-class families (e.g. local authority, or council, housing) by architects who are middle class. The architects have made the mistake of designing houses to suit their *own* conventions, rather than those of the people who will live in the houses. One example of this has been to pare down the space in the kitchen to a minimum, making it more like an efficient ship's galley. This might be fine for those middle-class families who appreciate having the separate dining room that this space saving makes possible, and who identify with the advertisers' images of efficient, space-saving, 'space-age' kitchens. But it is not

appreciated by the many working-class families who conventionally eat their meals in the kitchen, and for whom the kitchen is traditionally much more of a social place. For example, it is to the kitchen that neighbours, or the kids, might come for a cup of tea and a chat. Research workers have found that many families go to remarkable lengths to use their new, efficient kitchens in the old ways, for which they were not designed. Families will put up with a great deal of inconvenience in order, say, to cram a table and chairs into their tiny kitchen.

Exercise

You have just read an interesting, extended example of a point. What is that point? Put it into your own words (using the space below) and then refer back two paragraphs and underline the key phrases that express the point being made.

Discussion

The point is that there are 'subcultural differences in the way people use their homes': for example, 'there are subcultural differences between the various socio-economic classes'.

Figure 37 shows the plans of a two-storey house with (a) the furniture and general arrangements as envisaged by the architect who designed the house and (b) the actual furniture etc. as recorded by a research worker on a visit to the house when it was being lived in. There are considerable differences between the hypothetical and real uses of the house.

What important differences do you notice between the two plans in Figure 37?

The garage is not used for a car; the family perhaps does not own one. The 'dining room' is used as the general 'living room': it has a television in it, a settee and easy chairs as well as a dining table. The 'living room' seems to be reserved as a parlour for special occasions; it has the 'best' furniture. A drop-leaf table and two chairs are included in the kitchen, despite the fact that the position of the chair apparently makes it difficult to open the kitchen door. There is not enough storage space. A double bed, rather than the architect's 'neater' assumption of two single beds, is rather awkwardly placed in the second bedroom.

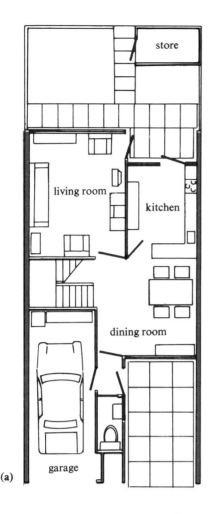

(a)

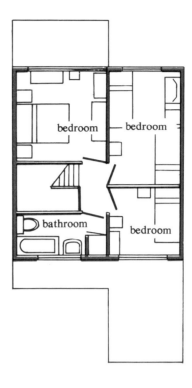

Figure 37 Plans of a two-storey council house: (a) with a furniture arrangement as originally envisaged by the architect; (b) the actual furniture in use, as recorded by a research observer

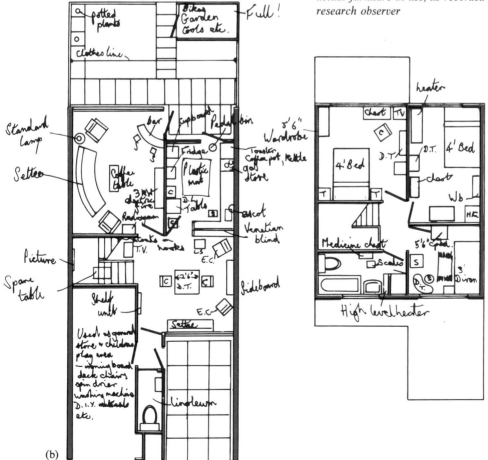

(b)

Despite the clear presence of social customs affecting Western house design, modern architects have tried to ignore such factors in favour of a so-called rational approach to interior planning. For instance, one of Le Corbusier's best-known slogans is that the house should be 'a machine for living in' (in a similar sense to that in which, say, an aeroplane is a machine for travelling in). The slogan expresses the apparent concern in twentieth-century Western culture for rationality and efficiency. Le Corbusier's attitude to interior planning is clearly expressed in his statement (made in 1929): 'The uses of the house consist in a regular sequence of definite functions. The regular sequence of these functions is a traffic phenomenon. To render that traffic exact, economical, and rapid, is the key effort of modern architectural science.'

This kind of rational, scientific (but nevertheless cultural) attitude to design was eventually adopted by most architects, if not by quite so many of the people who had to live in the 'machines' they designed. Do you, for example, really regard the life you live in your house as 'a regular sequence of definite functions'? Do you regard your movements about your house as 'a traffic phenomenon'?

There are serious shortcomings in the over-simplified attempts that emerged in the early part of this century to bring a rational attitude to the design of houses. It is quite impossible to remove completely all the socio-cultural, 'irrational' factors in design. For instance, is it rational to prefer a number of separate bedrooms as is the preference in the West, when other peoples sleep quite happily in one bedroom shared by all the family, or even shared by all the village?

However, there is now a tendency towards a culturally influenced attitude of rationality to many aspects of house design; people do not particularly want a house that is planned 'inconveniently'. This attitude towards convenient, rational design has helped architects to plan efficient layouts even in situations where their ingenuity has been taxed by the need to keep costs and space allocations to a minimum. This has been so particularly in the design of flats (see, for example, the flats designed by Le Corbusier, Figure 38) and in some special circumstances such as student study–bedrooms. A number of planning devices have been developed to help interior planning in these 'tight' situations, such as dual-purpose rooms (e.g. the bed–sittingroom), built-in furniture, circulation routes through rooms instead of through 'wasted' circulation space in corridors, and so on. In these situations architects have been helped by the availability of research data on minimum spatial requirements for typical activities in the home, such as eating around a table, making a bed, using the lavatory, etc.

The amount of space within a house often seems to the occupants to be rather limited; ideally, they would always like a larger house.

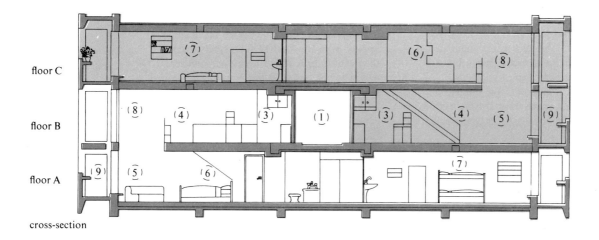

floor C

floor B

floor A

cross-section

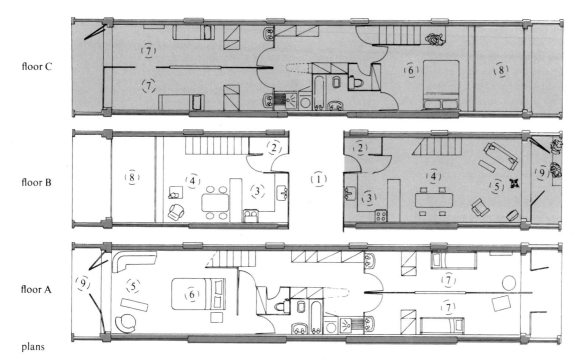

floor C

floor B

floor A

plans

Figure 38   This block of flats in Marseilles, France, was designed by Le Corbusier in 1946. He called the block a unité d'habitation; *the ideas it embodied were very influential with other architects. It demonstrates some ingenious devices of efficient but imaginative planning. The flats are entered from interior corridors. Each flat has a two-storey part and a single-storey part, with pairs of flats interlocking in section. Each flat is very thin and long, about 3.6 m (12 ft) by 18 m (60 ft), but a feeling of much greater spaciousness is created in the living area by its partial double height opening onto a balcony (see the interior photograph). This works particularly well for one of each pair of interlocking flats (the upper one in the section drawn), but not so well for the other one, in which the living room has to become a bed-sitting room. Notice how, typically for Le Corbusier, the service spaces* (bathrooms, lavatories, kitchens, etc.) are planned to minimum dimensions. He also relies quite a lot on built-in furniture to make his plans 'work', even to the extent of having bookshelves built into the walls and providing a built-in fold-away ironing board (broken outline on the plans). These devices help to make his versions of the furniture layouts look eminently reasonable, but they do reduce the occupants' freedom to replan their rooms more to their own preferences and needs. There are probably few people, for instance, who prefer to do their ironing in the hallway, even if this location is efficiently and conveniently near the drying and linen cupboards. Key: 1 access corridor, 2 entrance, 3 kitchen, 4 dining area, 5 living area, 6 main bedroom or bed area, 7 children's bedrooms, 8 open space to living area below, 9 balcony

This again is partly a new cultural tradition in the West. Over the last few hundred years expectations of how much room there should be in a house have risen progressively. However, apart from these social expectations, it is clear that there must be certain minimum space standards for certain activities; there is not a lot that you can do in a cupboard.

How can the size of space needed for various activities be determined?

If I take my own case, the activity I am engaged in now is writing this text. In order to 'house' this activity, I need space for my desk, my chair, and my bookshelves. So the sizes of these pieces of furniture set some minimum limits to the space I need. These minimum limits are increased by simple facts such as the need to move my chair so that I can seat myself at my desk and get up again, the need to move from my desk to my bookshelves, perhaps the need occasionally to pace the room, etc. There is also a minimum height to the space I need: at least my own height but preferably about 40–50 cm (16–20 inches) more (for throwing my arms up in despair, tearing my hair, jumping with excitement, etc.).

This simple procedure of checking my own requirements is fine as long as I am designing a space solely for myself, and just for one activity. But, usually, spaces have to be used for a variety of activities, and by a variety of people. It is then that designers need to know something of the typical sizes of furniture and equipment, and of the ranges of bodily sizes of the group of people they are designing for.

The various dimensions of the human body have been measured in statistical surveys. Making sure that the data collected in this way is reliable, and standardized, has led to the development of the science of *anthropometry*, a branch of *ergonomics* or *human factors*.

One area of house design where anthropometric data have been particularly applied is in the kitchen. This (and perhaps the bathroom) is where functional, efficient design is not only possible but also welcomed by many people, perhaps partly under the influence of the manufacturers of kitchen equipment, who have developed the image of the efficient kitchen to help sell their products. Anthropometric data can be used, for instance, to determine appropriate worktop and cupboard heights.

The kitchen is also the one place in the house where design analogies from industry, such as 'a regular sequence of definite functions', might be applicable. There are many aspects of cooking and food preparation that can be thought of as needing rational organization and functional space planning. For example, preparing a meal can be described in terms of a sequence of actions something like: taking raw food from storage (e.g. from the refrigerator), initial preparation (such as washing, peeling, mixing), putting into cooking container, placing in or on the cooker, removing from cooker, final preparation, serving. So the kitchen equipment could be planned in convenient locations for this sequence of activities, such as having a sequence of equipment: refrigerator, worktop, sink, worktop, cooker, worktop. This sequence allows the cook to move efficiently from one 'work-station' to the next as the food is sequentially processed from raw to prepared, cooked and served states.

Of course, not every aspect of house design, even in our 'rational' culture, can be regarded in such mechanistic terms. However, it is possible, and helpful to the designer, to think in terms of the sequence of major activities that occur in a house on a typical day. Figure 39 shows a typical 'diary' of family activities, as compiled in the Government design booklet *Space in the Home*.

Figure 39   A typical daily 'diary' of activities, for a family of two parents with three young children

0700   In the early morning rush, instant hot water and warmth are needed.

0710   Breakfast has to be served quickly, the school child got ready and the other children looked after as they wake up.

0830   Father and school child are off. Mother gives the other children their food and has something herself. A place where food can be eaten near the work area is useful.

0930 Mother puts the baby out in the pram and the toddler plays outside. The toddler wanders in and out of the house. Mother needs to be able to see the children easily while she works.

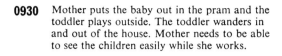

1130 Coming back from shopping loaded up, Mother needs space to put the pram and the shopping and elbow room to take off the children's outdoor clothes, and somewhere convenient to put them.

1200 When the children play indoors Mother needs to be able to see them from the kitchen, but they should be away from the kitchen equipment and not under her feet.

1230 When the family comes home to dinner on week days they have to wash and eat quickly. The dining space should be conveniently reached from the work centre.

1430 The baby needs a place where it is quiet to sleep. The toddler needs a place for play, where toys and other playthings can be concentrated, so the housewife does not have to be for ever tidying up.

1530 Space in the tidy area of the house is needed for adult visitors, while the children of both families play within sight but not too close to the teacups.

1700 Watching T.V. is a major family activity so the children come into the living room to watch.

1800 If people like watching T.V. while they are eating their evening meal, space for a low table is needed.

1830 People do not always want to watch T.V. when it is on, and need a place to sit away from it. The children need quiet when they are being settled down to sleep.

1900 When Father makes or repairs something, he needs to be out of Mother's way in the kitchen and where he will not disturb sleeping children.

2000 Sometimes visitors are being entertained while a child is watching his favourite T.V. programme.

2200 Mother may want to talk to visitors while she is preparing some snacks for them.

2330 The parents need to sleep near their young children, so that they can attend to them easily.

0300

It is often difficult to perceive the influence of one's own culture and values on things like house design because it is so obviously 'right'. The above 'daily diary' was abstracted from a government booklet originally published 20 years ago. Some cultural values and assumptions have changed since then. Spend a few minutes identifying the assumptions that might be different in a modern household and consider what, if any, implications the changes would have on the space requirements of the house.

From considering daily activities in this way, the designer can develop a number of commonsense features that help to make one plan more convenient than another. For instance, activities that are mutually incompatible (such as children's noisy play and adult's quiet reading) need plan arrangements that try to reduce the incompatibilities (for example, by putting the activities as far apart in the house as possible, or providing good sound insulation between rooms). A rather different situation might be the need to plan spaces in the house so that the play of babies and very young children can be observed by one or more adults while the adults are engaged in other activities (say, a parent working in the kitchen being able to keep an eye on a baby who is playing somewhere out of harm's way). With older children, such as teenagers or young adults, there is the converse need to provide them with a room where they can have some privacy away from their parents.

One way in which architects begin their design work, based on the consideration of future occupants' activities *before* actual rooms have been allocated, is to list a number of *activity spaces*. Each activity space represents the need for a space in which a certain activity is to be carried out: for

example, play space, cooking space, eating space, reading space, sleeping space. But this does not mean that each activity space will eventually be allocated its own separate room, since some activities may (for convenience or economy) share the same room.

Having listed the necessary activity spaces the designer can begin to consider how they might be arranged in relation to one another, by drawing a very abstract kind of 'plan' for the house. Such a plan is nothing more than a diagram in which the activity spaces are represented by small circles, joined together by link-lines to represent the fact that it would be desirable to have these linked activity spaces joined together in some way. So, for instance, if it would be desirable for the play space to be open to view from the cooking space, there would be a link drawn between these two; if it would be desirable to have the eating space opening directly from the cooking space, then those two would also be linked in the diagram.

The resulting *functional diagram* is an abstract model of the desired relations in the plan of the house. It suggests the way in which the spaces might be arranged, but it does not completely fix the future plan. Figure 40 shows that the same functional diagram may be transformed into many different architectural plans.

Sometimes the list of activity spaces can be quite long and the number of desired links can also be rather high. To help in deciding which links are desirable the architect might first use a systematic way of considering *all* the *possible* links. This is done by means of a chart that sets out all the possible interactions, or functional links, that could exist between the various activity spaces. Such a chart looks something like one of

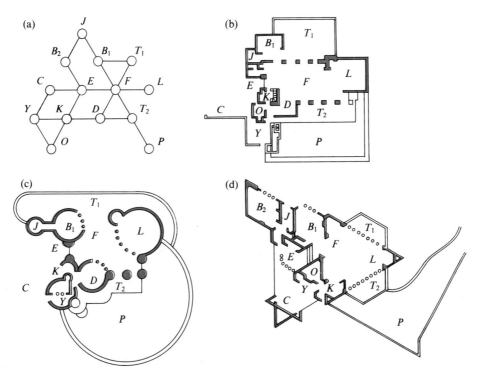

those mileage charts that show the distance between towns. Figure 41 shows a fairly simple example based on the functional diagram of Figure 40. This chart is called an *interaction matrix*. The word 'matrix' as used here means a grid set out in rows and columns. Each square (or 'cell') in the matrix represents the potential existence of a link between two rooms or spaces. Thus, in Figure 41 the left-hand column represents potential links between bedroom 1 and each other room or space: the first cell in that column represents the potential link between bedroom 1 and bedroom 2, the second cell represents that between bedroom 1 and the car port, and so on. Where a link actually is made in the functional diagram (and the resulting plans) this is shown by a dot entered in the appropriate cell of the matrix.

The interaction matrix is a 'model' of the house that is more abstract than a functional diagram; it is helpful in thinking systematically about every possible functional link that might exist between the activity spaces in the house. It can be used in more complex ways than the simple example of Figure 41, for instance by using numbers to represent the relative 'strength' of the desirability of having two spaces close together, or including a symbol for links that are definitely *not* wanted between two spaces.

Of course, not all the aspects of the design problem of planning a convenient house necessarily need *spatial* solutions, such as separate rooms for every activity. An alternative solution (that many people often have to adopt simply through lack of room) is to separate some activities in time, rather than in space; that is, by arranging domestic affairs so that incompatible activities do not compete for use of the same space at the same time.

Figure 40 A functional diagram is an abstract version of a house plan, which can represent many different actual or possible plans. The functional diagram here (a) has been shown to represent at least three different house plans designed by the American architect Frank Lloyd Wright. The plans are: (b) a 'House for a Family of $5000–$6000 income', designed as a project for Life *magazine in 1938; (c) the 'Ralph Jester house', Palos Verdes, California, 1938; (d) the 'Vigo Sundt house', near Madison, Wisconsin, 1941. Key: B_1 bedroom 1, B_2 bedroom 2 (Sundt house only), C car port, D dining room, E entrance, F family room, J bathroom, K kitchen, L living room, O office, P pool, T_1 terrace 1, T_2 terrace 2, Y yard*

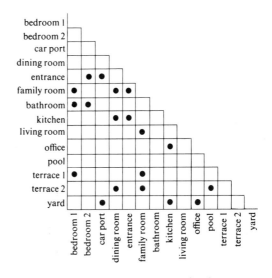

Figure 41 An interaction matrix for the Frank Lloyd Wright plans and the functional diagram of Figure 40. Each dot in a matrix cell represents a link drawn between activity spaces in the functional diagram

43

Figure 42 Planning in space and time: the first-floor apartment of the 'Schröder house' in Utrecht, Holland, designed by Gerrit Rietveld in 1923, has an arrangement of sliding walls that allow the plan to be divided into separate rooms or opened out into one large space, or variations between, to suit the needs and activities of the occupants. Plan (b) shows all the walls in place, providing a three-bedroom apartment; plan (c) shows all the walls folded away

Summary

Both functional and cultural factors influence the internal planning of a house. In Western culture the distinction between these factors has become blurred, as people have come to accept ideas of 'efficiency' and 'convenience' in house plans. Functional considerations often predominate in Western houses, but to some extent people still try to continue their customary patterns of living, even when their houses are designed to different patterns. Data and techniques are available to assist architects in the functional planning of rooms and equipment.

(a)

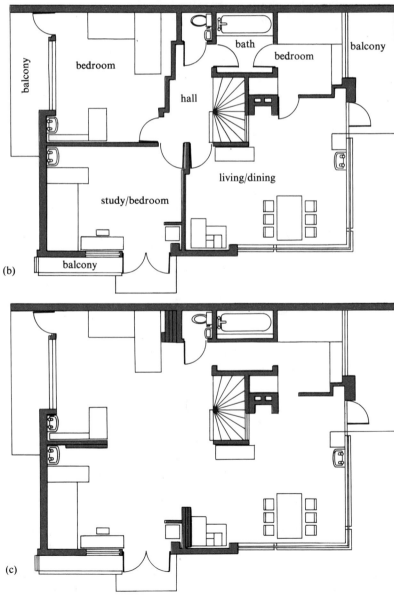

(b)

(c)

Activity 3   Relations between rooms

This activity is aimed at enabling you to analyse and evaluate your house plan in terms of its arrangement of spaces to suit your various domestic activities. It introduces you to ways of thinking about the house that use more abstract models than the scale plans. (Estimated activity time: about 1 hour.)

1   First draw a new, very diagrammatic plan of your house, in which each room is replaced by a small labelled circle placed roughly in the same location as it already exists. Where any of your rooms is clearly used for more than one activity (e.g. cooking and dining, or dining and living) give it separate circles for each activity. Include in this diagrammatic plan separate circles for separate circulation areas, such as corridors and halls.

2   Now draw in link-lines between the circles for each case where it is possible in your existing house to move directly from one room or space to another. That is, if there is a door between two rooms, or between a room and a corridor, or if two or more spaces share the same room, then it is possible to move directly from one to the other, so draw in a link-line. Also draw in links to the exterior where rooms have such access. It may be easier (or neater) to draw this diagram if you rearrange the locations of some of the circles. If you have more than one floor in your house, connected by a staircase, it would also be correct to draw in a link-line between the spaces on each floor that are connected by the staircase. As you can see in my example, I redrew the diagrams to make the links clear, without worrying whether the relative geographical relationships of the spaces stayed the same.

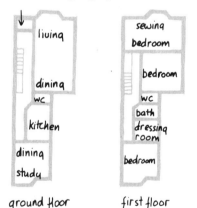

My house plan

Most rooms have one major function - but the back ground-floor room is used both as study and dining room. The front room is also occasionally used for dining as well as living. My wife uses the front bedroom for sewing and quilt-making - special equipment, so space is needed

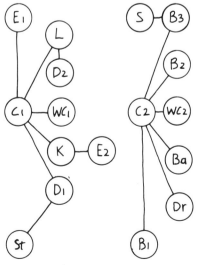

My house plan represented diagrammatically as activity spaces.

Key:

St	—	study
D	—	dining
K	—	kitchen
L	—	living
B	—	bedroom
Dr	—	dressing room
Ba	—	bathroom
S	—	sewing
C	—	circulation
E₁	—	exterior (front)
E₂	—	exterior (rear)
WC	—	lavatory

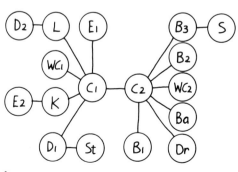

'Functional diagram' of my house

45

You now have a functional diagram of your house, showing the activity spaces it contains and the way in which they are linked for access to one another. It can be a more useful model in some ways than the scale plans you drew in Activity 2. For instance, it allows you to think about the existence of, and the need for or desirability of, direct access between one room and another, without being limited by the concrete reality of the existing plan. This functional diagram represents your home as it is arranged at the moment. We shall now go on to consider whether this arrangement is as you would like it to be, or whether there might be some more convenient arrangement.

3 To do this you need a way of thinking systematically about the functional links between all the activity spaces. I want you to be able to think about every possible link that might be made, so that you can ask yourself whether or not you would really like such a link to be made. The way to do this is to use an interaction matrix.

A blank matrix is provided for you to fill in. Down the side and along the bottom of the matrix write in the names of each of the activity spaces you included in your functional diagram. The order in which you write them is not important. You can refer to the matrix I filled in for my house, as an example.

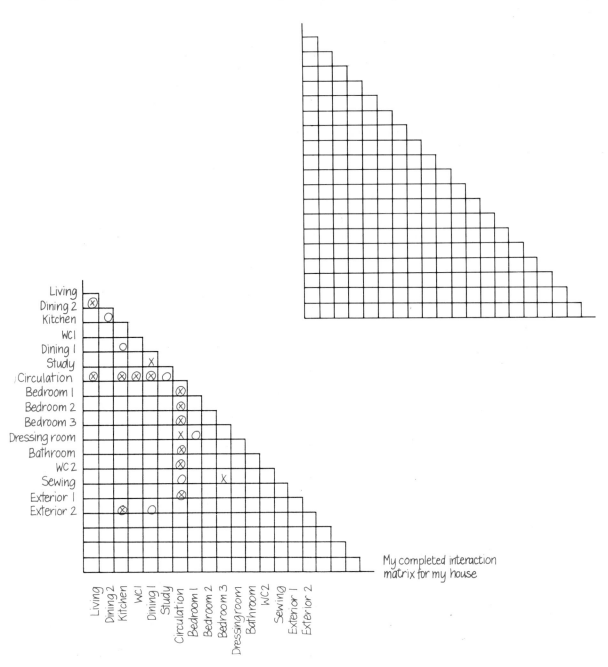

My completed interaction matrix for my house

Very carefully, go down each column in your own matrix and at each cell ask yourself these questions:

In my current house plan, is there a direct link between these two spaces? You should be able to check back to your functional diagram for confirmation of your answer. If there is a link, it should be drawn as a line in the diagram. If your answer is 'yes', then mark the cell with a cross.

Would I *like* to have a direct link between these two spaces, whether or not one exists at present? If your answer to this question is 'yes', then mark the cell with a circle. Otherwise, leave the cell blank.

Probably, where a link already exists, you will want to keep it, but sometimes you won't want to. For instance, I don't really want to keep the link between study and dining spaces in my back room, I would rather they were separate. And in a few cases, maybe, you would like a link to exist where there is none at present; say from the dining room to the back garden ('exterior 2' in the matrix) in my case, where French windows into the garden would be nice.

When you have completed the matrix you should be able to see quite clearly where you have undesirable links in your current plan (the un-circled crosses in the matrix cells) and where currently non-existent links would in fact be desirable (the plain circles).

4   You can now use the matrix as a guide in redrawing your functional diagram so that it represents your house plan as you would *like* it to be. Draw a new functional diagram that includes all those links that have a circle in their matrix cell and leave out those that only have a cross.

Of course, this functional diagram shows only the theoretical links that might exist in your preferred house plan; it might not be possible in practice to make the links you desire, given the restrictions of your existing house plan. In theory, provided that it is possible to draw the functional diagram in such a way that no links cross, then it is possible to construct a plan so that all the linking conditions are satisfied, but it might mean a totally different house plan to the one that you already have.

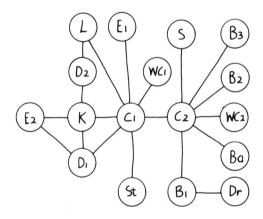

A revised functional diagram for my house, based on the interaction matrix

8 Keeping warm

This section is closely related to Sections 1 and 2 of Block 1 *Heat*. You might like to study those sections before continuing with this section. Alternatively, you could leave studying the tributary as a whole until you reach the end of this section. The later parts of the tributary are concerned with the detailed calculation of the amount of heat required to keep a home comfortably warm.

Perhaps a more basic purpose of a house than the provision of 'convenient' accommodation is that it should provide sheltered accommodation. By this, I mean that the house provides shelter against the rigours of the natural environment.

The natural environment is often inhospitable, or certainly less comfortable than people prefer: it is frequently too hot, or too cold, or too wet, etc. This suggests that there is some kind of 'comfort zone' within which people prefer to live: a zone of limited ranges for the various aspects of climate that humans are capable of sensing, such as temperature. Can we establish what these 'comfort' levels are? This is what I shall be trying to do in the beginning of this section, considering particularly temperature and humidity. Later in the section I shall be dealing especially with heat in the home, as this is perhaps the major comfort factor. You will be learning some general principles of how the need to keep comfortably warm can influence the design of a house, including its shape, orientation and building materials.

It is in fact very difficult to reach universal agreement on the meaning of 'comfort'; usually the best that can be done is to define it as an absence of discomfort. It is *dis*comfort that I feel when I say I am too hot or too cold. There are also considerable differences between the levels at which people begin to feel uncomfortable. Partly this is due to 'acclimatization', that is, adaptation by one's body to the climate it is used to. People moving from one part of the world to another with a very different climate can feel uncomfortable for many months, or even years, until their interior body mechanisms have adjusted to the changed external conditions. Also there may be some physiological differences between races that make people of one race more comfortable in some climates than in others.

However, there are even significant differences in 'comfort' levels for people of the same race, in the same place, on the same day. For example, women tend to prefer a slightly higher temperature (about 1 °C) than men, and older people (over forty years of age) also prefer a slightly higher temperature than do younger people. The time of year makes a difference, too: people feel comfortable at higher temperatures in summer than they do in winter.

There are a number of factors that can be identified as contributing to a basic feeling of comfort, but the two principal factors are usually temperature and humidity. Temperature is a measure of heat (how 'hot' the air is) and is usually measured in degrees Celsius (also called degrees centigrade) or, sometimes still in Britain, degrees Fahrenheit. Humidity is a measure of the moisture content of the air (how 'damp' it is).

There are two ways in which humidity can be measured. *Absolute humidity* is the amount of water vapour actually present in a given volume of air, measured in grams per cubic centimetre. *Relative humidity* is the absolute humidity expressed as a percentage of the amount of water vapour needed to saturate the air. When the air is at 100% relative humidity, it is completely saturated with water vapour, and the vapour begins to condense as fine droplets of mist or fog, or to form dew on cold surfaces. So the nearer to 100% the relative humidity is, the wetter the air feels. On a hot, humid day you might feel 'sticky'; your perspiration is less able to evaporate because there is already a high percentage of moisture in the air. How much moisture the air can hold before the moisture condenses depends on the air temperature: the warmer the air is, the more moisture it can hold. This explains why condensation forms on cold surfaces, such as window panes. The air temperature drops significantly against the window pane and its relative humidity therefore rises, to 100% for condensation to form.

For Europeans the comfort range for air temperature is about 18–24 °C (65–75 °F), and the comfort range for relative humidity is about 40–70%. However, what is 'comfortable' also depends very much on what you are doing at the time; strenuous physical activity needs a much lower air temperature for comfort than does sitting in a deck-chair. Figure 43 shows in very simplified form the 'comfort zone' for sedentary activity, in terms of temperature and humidity.

Obviously temperature and humidity out of doors in Britain will often fall within the comfort zone shown in Figure 43 and so (if the other factors that influence comfort, such as air movement, are also within comfort limits) at those times it is quite possible to be comfortable out of doors without any shelter. However, as you well know, the number of days in a year on which all the comfort factors are satisfied is actually rather few in Britain. So, for a comfortable life, shelter from the elements is needed for most of the year in Britain. A simple shelter would provide some protection (principally against wind and rain) and would be adequate for the few summer months, but for the rest of the year not only is shelter needed but also some more active forms of modifiers of the climate, particularly some form of heating.

How do you heat your house? Probably by burning a fuel such as coal, gas or oil, or by 'burning' electricity. (Clearly, electricity is not a fuel like the others, and it is not literally burnt even in an electric fire. But people do often talk of 'burning electricity', obviously equating it with their use of other fuels.)

You know which fuel you use, but do you know how much heat you use to keep your house at a comfortable temperature? If you use 5 tonnes of coal a year in your fireplaces and your neighbour used 1500 litres of oil for his central heating system, which of you is using more heat? To answer such a question it is necessary to be able to convert quantities of various fuels (tonnes of coal, litres of oil, cubic metres of gas, etc.) to a common standard unit of heat. It is not adequate simply to compare the monetary costs of the various fuels, because these costs are subject to many influences, as with the oil price rises of recent years, and even if you burn logs that you pick up for free in the local woods you are still clearly using heat, if not money, to keep your house warm.

The unit of heat that is used by technologists in order to compare the heat energy contained in different fuels is the *gigajoule* (whose symbol is GJ). Table 1 gives the number of gigajoules used by an average British household in a year not only for heating but also for cooking, lighting and running the various household appliances such as radios and televisions, refrigerators and vacuum cleaners.

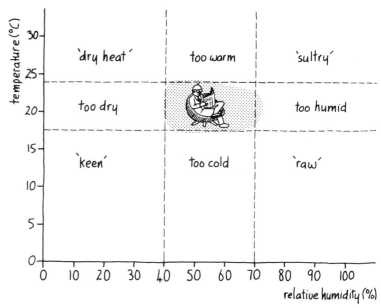

Figure 43 The 'comfort zone' in terms of temperature and humidity for sedentary activity and people's subjective responses to various climatic conditions outside that zone

Table 1 Annual energy use by an average British household (1988)

	Fuel use	Percentage
space heating (fires, central-heating boilers, etc.)	51.0 GJ	60%
hot water	19.6 GJ	23%
cooking	6.0 GJ	7%
lights	3.4 GJ	4%
appliances	5.0 GJ	6%
Total	85.0 GJ	100%

So far I have considered house heating only in terms of burning fuels, or the use of *purposive sources* as they have been called, sources that are purposely designed and used primarily to provide heat. There are also *incidental sources* of heat gain in a house. The sun is one major 'incidental' contributor. People are another. People give off heat, and the more of them you can cram into your house the less you will need other sources of heat, as you may have noticed at a crowded party. Household appliances are also incidental sources of heat. A refrigerator, for example, gives off some incidental heat, so does a television set and other electrical appliances, and there is always 'waste' heat from cooking.

Perhaps because the sun is a rather unreliable source in Britain, conventional house design has tended to ignore it. However, you may have noticed that some houses, or some rooms in a house, are more of a 'sun-trap' than others. Because of their *orientation* (particularly that of their windows) towards the sun they pick up significant quantities of solar heat on sunny days. This orientation *could* be used more deliberately in house design, although there are often other, overriding factors such as the need to fit a group of houses on to a restricted site, or to build terraces on either side of a road, and so on. It is nevertheless possible to consider the overall shape of a house and its orientation on an idealized open site and to reach conclusions on the best design that is suited to a particular climate.

In his book *Design with Climate* (Princeton University Press, 1963), Victor Olgyay has suggested that four basic house forms can be considered, corresponding to four principal types of climate: cold, temperate, hot-arid and hot-humid (Figure 44). In cold regions the need to conserve heat is very important and leads to trying to minimize the outer surface area of the house, in order to reduce heat loss. This minimum surface area is in fact achieved in the hemispherical form of the igloo, although for other materials and in less severe conditions it is usually more practical to aim for a cube-like shape for the house. In temperate regions (such as Britain) a rectangular plan is desirable, with the shorter sides facing east and west. Such a house has a long southern face, which catches the solar heat when it is available. Because the climate is not so extreme, however, more diversity in house shapes is possible in temperate regions without significantly affecting heat gain or loss. In hot-arid (desert) regions the extreme conditions demand a return to a more compact shape, with the addition of special features such as internal shaded courtyards cooled by water to help create a comfortable 'micro-climate' within the house and its immediate surroundings. In hot-humid

(tropical forest and swamp) regions the actual temperature is usually not so excessive as in hot-arid regions, but the high humidity significantly affects discomfort. So long as the roof provides adequate shelter against rain and sun, an open-sided elongated shape has the advantage of being able to catch any cooling breezes.

The orientation of the house is obviously important for elongated shapes. Other factors (e.g. wind direction, access) can be just as, or more, important in planning the orientation of the house, but usually the dominant factor is the orientation of the main facade towards the sun. In temperate regions this is a matter of trying to arrange the house shape and orientation so as to collect as much heat as possible from the sun in winter, while avoiding overheating from solar gain in the summer. In the northern temperate regions the maximum summer solar gain in fact comes from a south-westerly direction, whereas the maximum winter solar gain comes from slightly east of south. These comments apply to the whole house, not just to window orientation, and to the build-up of heat during the whole day. This conveniently means that, in temperate regions, the optimum orientation for the longer facade is just to the east of south so as to receive the most winter warmth, thereby turning the shorter facade to the south-west, the direction of highest solar gain in summer (Figure 45).

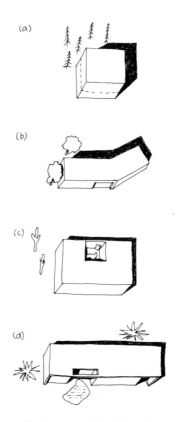

Figure 44   Four basic building shapes suited to four distinct kinds of climate: (a) cold, (b) temperate, (c) hot-arid and (d) hot-humid

50

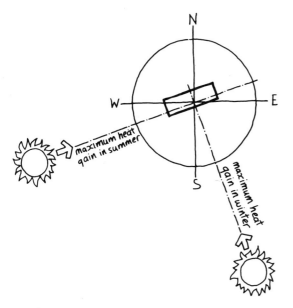

Figure 45 *The best orientation for the longer facade of a house in a northern temperate region is slightly to the east of south, to take advantage of solar gain in winter while avoiding overheating in summer*

Changing the orientation of a house plan can have a major effect on how much solar heat it might gain. In one orientation a house can be overheated by the sun in summer, yet get little or no benefit from the sun in winter; in a different orientation the same house design can be picking up maximum solar gain in the winter, while not becoming overheated in summer.

To understand how this change of orientation can be so significant, you need to know something of the sun's movements in the sky (Figure 46). In Britain in midsummer, the sun rises in the north-east and sets in the north-west and at midday reaches an angle overhead of approximately 60° to the horizontal. In midwinter, it rises in the south-east and sets in the south-west, and at midday reaches an angle of only 15° to the horizontal. Between midsummer and midwinter the apparent path of the sun varies between these extremes.

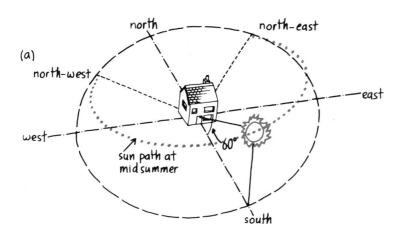

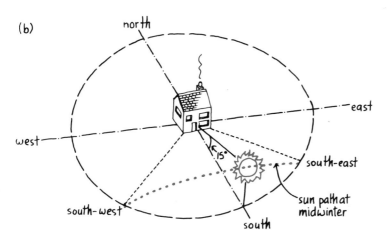

Figure 46 *The apparent movement of the sun through the sky at (a) midsummer and (b) midwinter over central Britain*

As an example of design for orientation, in the hypothetical house in Figure 47 the living room and bedroom 1 face south-west in orientation (a) and gain the maximum midsummer solar heat, but in midwinter they receive the setting sun too late in the day to gain much benefit from it. In orientation (b) the living room and bedroom 1 face south-east and receive the morning sun, which helps to warm the house in midwinter, but doesn't become too hot in summer. The loggia roof shades the main living-room windows from the hottest south and south-westerly sun in midsummer, but in midwinter the sun is lower in the sky and therefore penetrates below the shading angle of the roof. Also, in orientation (b) the dining room and kitchen pick up the late-evening summer sun in the north-west, which might be welcome, and both bedrooms receive early-morning sun for most of the year.

There is one other design factor that is important in modifying the internal environment of the house relative to the external environment and that is the actual *material* of which the house is built. The particular building materials used can have a profound effect on internal temperature, especially. This is because, although certain materials can keep out certain climatic elements such as rain and wind completely, there is no material that can completely prevent heat passing through it, so whenever there is a difference between the external air temperature and the air temperature inside the house there is a flow of heat from the one to the other, through the walls. The rate of heat flow is different for different materials, and this partly explains why some buildings heat up quite quickly in hot weather and also cool down quite quickly in cold weather, whereas others take much longer.

Can you think of any examples?

In general, massive types of construction are much slower to transmit heat than lighter ones. Thus a thick-walled stone-built church feels cool inside even on a hot day, whereas, say, a light timber shed will heat up quite quickly.

Figure 47   The same plan in two different orientations. In orientation (a) it is cold in winter and hot in summer; in orientation (b) it is warm in winter and cool in summer. The loggia roof overhang shades the main living-room glazing in summer, but does not obscure the lower-angled winter sun

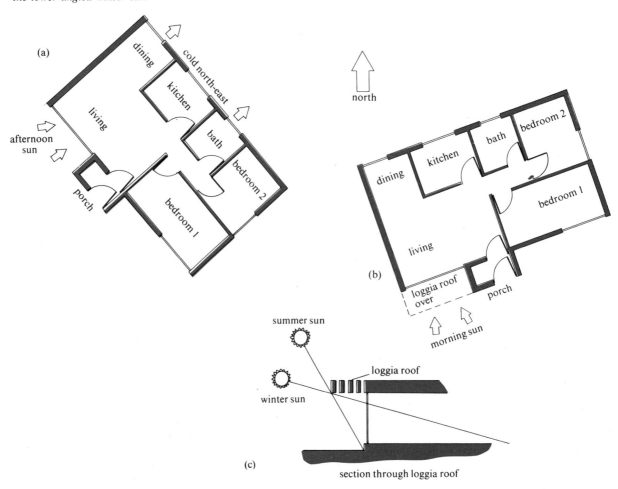

This *thermal conductivity* is a property of materials that makes some of them good insulators against heat transmission while others are poor insulators. Thick-walled buildings of heavy construction also have a high *thermal capacity*, that is, heat is 'stored' in the walls (like in the bricks inside a 'storage heater') and is only absorbed or released quite slowly. This is used to advantage in, for example, thick heavy earth-walled houses, such as the pueblo, in hot-arid climates. The houses warm up only slowly during the hot day, so feeling relatively cool inside, and then slowly release the stored heat during the cold night, so feeling relatively warm inside. In temperate regions lighter forms of construction are generally preferred, of lower thermal capacity, so that the warmth of the sun is quickly absorbed whenever it is available. Very lightweight forms of construction are preferred in hot-humid climates, so avoiding any temperature build-up in the house, which would have an associated higher humidity, and offering instead a shady, well-ventilated, cooler internal environment.

The *colour* of a material is also influential in its absorption of heat. Dark colours absorb heat more readily than lighter ones, which reflect more of the heat. This is one reason why the *trullo* builders, and other people who live in bright, hot regions, whitewash their walls and roofs.

The fact that no material is actually impervious to heat flow, that is, does not completely prevent heat flowing, explains why you need to *keep* pumping heat into your house in order to maintain a comfortable temperature. Whenever there is a temperature difference between the inside and outside of your house, then heat inevitably flows from the warmer to the cooler; when it is cold outside heat is continually flowing out through your house walls. And not only through your walls but also through the roof, floor, doors and windows. Figure 48 shows the typical percentage losses through the various house surfaces. This heat loss is a fact of life, I'm afraid, and the best you can do is to improve the insulation of your house so that the rate of heat loss is *slowed*, but it can never be stopped altogether.

Once again, the shape of the house can be important. A cube, for instance, is more compact than a long, thin, rectangular box; it has less surface area in proportion to the volume it contains and, if there is less surface area, then there is less heat loss. A detached house has all its external walls facing the cold outside world, and so loses heat through all of them, whereas a semi-detached house is better off: one wall faces the neighbouring semi-detached, which is presumably being kept at about the same temperature by its occupants, so there is no heat loss at all

either way through that wall. A house in the middle of a terrace is even better off.

Sections 3, 4 and 5 of the Block 1 *Heat* tributary explain the basis of the heat load calculation that will be used in the design task described in Part Three of this mainstream text. This includes discussing the roles of different materials, internal and solar gains and how these all combine together in the overall calculation. If you haven't already done so, this is a good time to break off and study Block 1 *Heat*.

Summary

It is impossible to be precise in defining a 'comfortable' environment. However, for thermal comfort it is possible to specify temperature ranges within which people generally feel comfortable, depending on what they are doing and wearing, how old they are, what temperatures they may be used to, etc. In a temperate or cool climate, such as Britain's, internal space heating is necessary to maintain a comfortable level of warmth. Space heating accounts for about 60% of the total fuels used for various purposes in a typical British household. As well as burning fuel as a purposive source of heat, there are also incidental sources. A major 'incidental' source is the sun, but British houses are not usually designed with the best form and orientation to take advantage of solar heat gain. Heat flows into and out of a house because no material completely stops heat flow, although different materials have different thermal conductivities, which affect the rates of heat flow.

Figure 48 Typical heat losses through the various surfaces etc. of a house, shown as percentages of the total heat loss

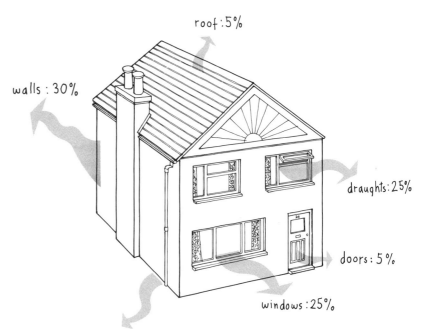

roof : 5%

walls : 30%

draughts : 25%

doors : 5%

windows : 25%

floor : 10%

In this course (and in most technology courses) diagrams, drawings, photographs and illustrations of various kinds are used as an integral part of the teaching material. You should make sure that you *read* the illustrations with the same care that you read the text.

Exercise

Look back over the illustrations in this section. Think about the *nature* of each illustration – what kind of information or idea it is conveying. See if you can understand the significance of each illustration and how it relates to the ideas developed in the text. Consider why the author has included each illustration, and whether it might have been possible or preferable to have conveyed the ideas in words.

Discussion

Each of the illustrations in this section is of a different type, although several of them may look rather similar.

The first illustration, Figure 43, conveys in a simple visual form a lot of *data* and related information about people's responses to temperature and relative humidity. To convey the same information in words only would have taken a lengthy and complicated piece of text, and it's almost certain that you would not have grasped the information as readily as you can from the illustration. Notice how the shaded area implies that the 'comfort zone' is less well-defined than might be suggested by the rigid rectangle enclosed by the dotted lines. The drawing inside the zone also implies the kind of activity for which this zone is 'comfortable'.

Figure 44 is a different kind of illustration. It doesn't really convey any more information than the text alongside it, but it shows *examples* of the types of building forms that are outlined in the text. It therefore makes the text easier to understand. You might also find the pictures easier to remember than the words in the text.

The next illustration, Figure 45, is a graphical representation of some *principles* that are also explained in the text. The drawing enables you literally to 'see' what the author means; how the two important orientations happen to come conveniently at right-angles to each other.

Figure 46 is a *visualization* of something that happens in three-dimensional space and time – the apparent motion of the sun through the sky. Once again, the illustration easily conveys something that is much more difficult to convey with words alone; notice

how the textual explanation is very brief and relies on your reading of the illustration.

Figure 47 adopts some of the conventions of a *technical illustration* – in this case an architect's drawings for describing the layout of a house. The plan of a building would be almost impossible to convey to someone else in words alone.

Like the first illustration in the section, the 'comfort zone' graph, Figure 48 also conveys *data* in a graphical form, although not in the standardized format of a graph. In this case the data are the various percentage figures of heat loss, presented in a directly representational form. Notice how the arrows are drawn to different thicknesses to suggest the relative amounts of heat loss.

These different kinds of illustration make their points clearly and vividly. They convey ideas and information that are not easy to convey by words alone, and they help you to understand the text. They are not there just to make the book look more attractive! Since technology is so often about real-world objects, illustrations are used in technology courses to explain those objects, and also to help you to 'visualize' the ideas connected with those objects. In your study notes and assignments remember that you can use illustrations yourself to help convey ideas and information.

You might like to look back over the other illustrations that have appeared so far, and consider what kind of job each one is doing. And as a final exercise you might like to think about how the data in Table 1 of this section (on page 49) might have been conveyed in an illustration, and try drawing your own illustration for it.

Activity 4   Shape and orientation

The purpose of this activity is to help you to assess how well your house has been shaped and oriented to take account of the sun's apparent 'movement' around it. (Estimated activity time: about ½ hour.)

1   Draw an outline plan of your house, showing just the external walls but clearly distinguishing between solid walls and windows. If you have neighbouring houses attached to yours (e.g. semi-detached or terraced) or in very close proximity, show those in outline too. (See my example.)

2   If you don't already know where north is in relation to your house, then find out by observing either a compass or the sun (see Figure 46; the simplest way is to note that the sun is to the south at noon). Draw a north-point on your plan and then indicate the major sun orientations: sunrise and sunset at midsummer and midwinter (approximately 45° to north and south in each case). For the major windows, plot how the sun falls through them (not forgetting the shading effects of the neighbouring houses or other obstructions).

3   How good or bad is the orientation to the sun of your house? Do some windows act as convenient sun-traps for winter sun, or do they trap too much sun in summer? Do neighbouring houses block the sun? Are they perhaps better oriented than yours? What about the overall shape of your house: is it anything near the best shape for a temperate climate (see Figure 44)? Could the orientation have been improved if the house had been twisted slightly on its site?

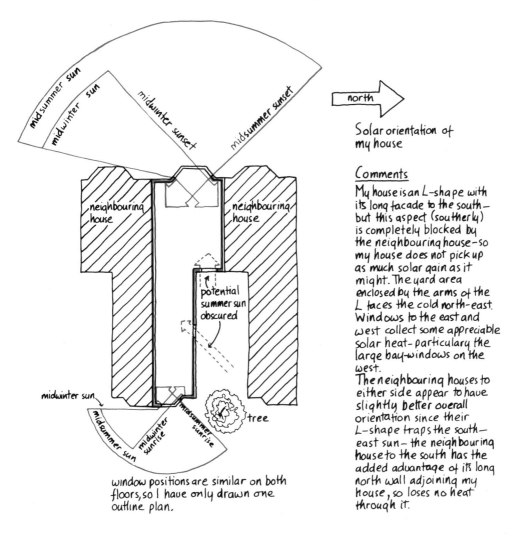

Solar orientation of my house

Comments

My house is an L-shape with its long facade to the south — but this aspect (southerly) is completely blocked by the neighbouring house — so my house does not pick up as much solar gain as it might. The yard area enclosed by the arms of the L faces the cold north-east. Windows to the east and west collect some appreciable solar heat — particulary the large bay-windows on the west.

The neighbouring houses to either side appear to have slightly better overall orientation since their L-shape traps the south-east sun — the neighbouring house to the south has the added advantage of its long north wall adjoining my house, so loses no heat through it.

window positions are similar on both floors, so I have only drawn one outline plan.

55

9 The influence of services

'...one must observe a fundamental difference between environmental aids of the structural type (including clothes) and those of which the camp-fire is the archetype. Let the difference be expressed in a form of parable, in which a savage tribe (of the sort that exists only in parables) arrives at an evening camp-site and finds it well supplied with fallen timber. Two basic methods of exploiting the environmental potential of that timber exist: either it may be used to construct a wind-break or rain-shed – the structural solution – or it may be used to build a fire – the power-operated solution. An ideal tribe of noble rationalists would consider the amount of wood available, make an estimate of the probable weather for the night – wet, windy, or cold – and dispose of its timber resources accordingly. A real tribe, being the inheritors of ancestral cultural predispositions would do nothing of the sort, of course, and would either make fire or build a shelter according to prescribed custom...' (Reyner Banham, *The Architecture of the Well-tempered Environment*, Architectural Press, 1969, pp. 18–19.)

To this parable one might add that people who live in climates that are generally rather cool (such as in Britain), seem traditionally to need both options: to build a shelter and then to light a fire inside it. In the previous section I was largely concerned with what Banham categorized as the 'structural solution' to creating a comfortable environment, that is with the shape, orientation and materials of a house. This way of viewing a house design is to see it as essentially a *passive* device for modifying the environment: the building stands passively as a barrier between the internal and external environments, or as a collector of solar heat. However, it is usually necessary to add more *active* means of environmental control in order to achieve preferred comfort levels, that is, to adopt what Banham categorized as the 'power-operated solution'. An active or power-operated environmental modifier might be nothing more than an open fire to warm the air inside the shelter, but it could obviously extend to a fully air-conditioned environment.

Thus the provision of building *services* (including not only heat, but also light, ventilation, power, water and drainage) can have a profound effect on house design. The designer has to consider the balance between the active and passive elements at his

disposal, integrating a power-based solution with a structural solution. In this section I shall rather briefly introduce and review the design effects of building services, each of which could, and does, form a major area of technological study in its own right.

The author has just summarized his main aim for this section, but notice that there has already been quite a long introductory statement in which he made what seems to be a key distinction between *active* and *passive* means of maintaining a comfortable environment.

If you haven't already done so, try quickly surveying the rest of this section to see how the main point of the 'influence of services' is developed. Then try making a 'spray' or 'tree' diagram of the points and subpoints during your study of the section.

The need to heat one's house in the British climate has had quite a strong influence on the traditional house plan. A dominating presence in the plans of vernacular British houses is the large fireplace. The plans are often just one or two rooms built around a fireplace (Figure 49).

In the simplest case the fire 'place' is merely an open hearth located somewhere near the centre of the main (and perhaps the only) room. In these early house designs the smoke from the fire escaped (as best it could) through windows and doors and by filtering through the roof, but in later designs the fireplace becomes fixed in position by providing for it a chimney, usually built into one of the walls. The importance of the fire's place in the house is nevertheless still clear, and easy to understand when you remember that the fire was probably the only source not only of heat for cooking and keeping occupants warm, but also of light.

Today, the fireplace has lost much, and in some cases all, of its importance. The modern householder has a choice of heating systems, in many of which the conventional fireplace is redundant. At the absolute extreme (but perhaps beyond the financial means of any mere householder) it is possible to have a totally power-operated and controlled environment, even using 'air curtains' to 'enclose' a space within which almost any desired environmental condition could be maintained by mechanical means.

The conventional European house lies between the extremes of totally passive and

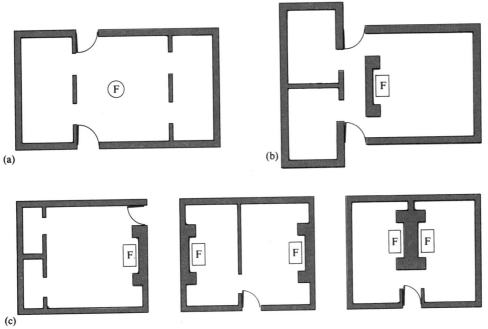

(a)

(b)

(c)

Figure 49   The central importance of the fireplace in vernacular British house plans:
(a) early 'hall' plan with central open fireplace; (b) later 'hall' plan with chimney;
(c) variations on the basic 'two-unit' cottage

Figure 50   The 'environment-bubble'; a design concept for the ultimate 'power-operated' house, proposed by Reyner Banham in 1965. The 'house' is a plastic inflatable dome containing a single, multi-function integrated services module

THE ENVIRONMENT-BUBBLE
TRANSPARENT PLASTIC BUBBLE DOME INFLATED BY AIR-CONDITIONING OUTPUT

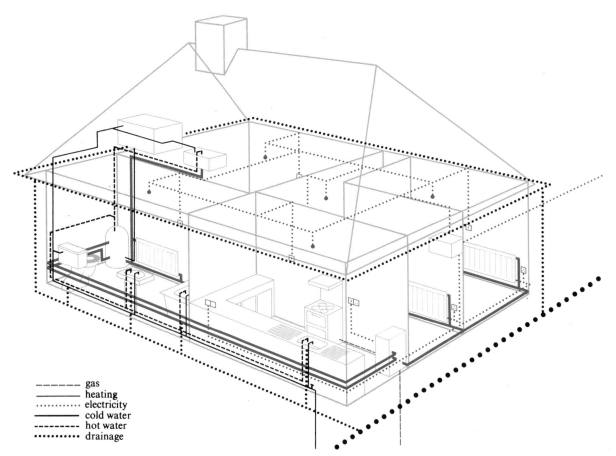

```
----------- gas
_____ heating
··········· electricity
▬▬▬▬▬▬▬▬▬ cold water
----------- hot water
●●●●●●●●●●● drainage
```

Figure 51   A view of a typical house, showing the many service pipes, cables, etc. that are usually hidden

totally active environmental control devices. Its structure has a large passive role to play in keeping out wind and rain, but it also places a considerable reliance on more active services components, especially fires or other heating devices. Because it is more than a simple shelter, and provides a variety of supporting devices for domestic life such as heating, cooking, lighting, communication, washing and lavatory installations, it contains quite a complex set of services. A picture which emphasizes these usually hidden services rather than the more visible structure of a house is reminiscent of a diagram of the nerves, arteries, etc. of a human body (Figure 51).

In fact the total service installations in a new house represent a significant fraction of the overall cost of the house, about 10–15%. This means that there is usually some concern to plan these installations into the house as economically as possible. This need to plan economically is one of the major constraints through which building services influence plan form and interior layouts.

For instance, it is usually desirable to keep the more highly serviced rooms close together in the plan, so that there is little or no duplication of service installations, pipe runs, etc. This is one reason why bathrooms and kitchens are usually adjacent (whether side by side or one above the other) in house plans,

although there are usually no other reasons of planning convenience why they should be together. However, there is another important constraint in the provision of drainage services (i.e. wastes from sinks, baths and lavatories) that also causes these services to be clustered together. This is the constraint on the possible geometric arrangements of drainage pipe runs; especially on the limiting distance that a fitting (say, a lavatory) can be placed from the central stack drain-pipe to which the drainage outlets from the house are connected.

These kinds of constraint imply that it is usually not possible to place serviced rooms simply anywhere in a plan. In general, therefore, the serviced rooms are clustered together. This can be a particularly important aspect in the planning of multi-storey flats, where the cost of the service installations might rise considerably if the serviced rooms were not clustered quite compactly, both horizontally on each floor and vertically from floor to floor. (You might like to refer back to the plans of Le Corbusier's *Unité d'Habitation* flats, Figure 38, to see this clustering in practice.)

The economic and geometric constraints on water and waste services are very similar to those of providing fireplaces and chimneys. In the most primitive cases the fireplace fulfils the function of a camp-fire: it is the central (and only) source of heat and light. Later vernacular house plans show the one or two warm rooms clustered around a central fireplace.

Figure 52 (a) The 'Robie house', Chicago, USA, designed by Frank Lloyd Wright in 1910. (b) Schematic plan of main floor; (c) section through living room; (d) plan of living room and dining room. An example of innovative architectural design which took advantage of 'power-operated' solutions to environmental control and integrated them with more traditional 'passive' design solutions. The main floor (b and d) is virtually an open-plan design, although living and dining areas are separated by a central staircase and fireplace, the latter being principally 'ceremonial' or psychological in function, rather than a necessary heating source. This large and grand living space is almost entirely walled with windows providing natural light and also, since almost all the glazing is openable, plentiful ventilation, which is necessary in Chicago's summers. Around this glazed perimeter Wright provided for a complete heating skirt, with radiators built into the wall panels below the windows and let into the floor beneath the french windows opening onto the south-facing terrace.

Wright went further than this in his control of the environment, by his attention to details such as the installation of the electric lights, which are integrated with the building structure and finishes. One set of lights are frosted-glass globes around the perimeter of the central raised portion of the ceiling. But lighting the perimeter 'aisle' of the lower ceiling level is a set of dimmer-controlled lamps let into the ceiling and casting a dappled light through decorative grilles. These grilles also act as vents to allow air to be drawn into the roof-space and out through a ventilating chimney.

Key: 1 roof overhang, 2 opening windows, 3 glazed doors, 4 roof space, 5 radiators under windows, 6 radiators sunk in floor, 7 glass lighting globes, 8 structural steel beam, 9 dimmer-controlled bulbs, 10 lighting grilles, 11 hinged fly-screens

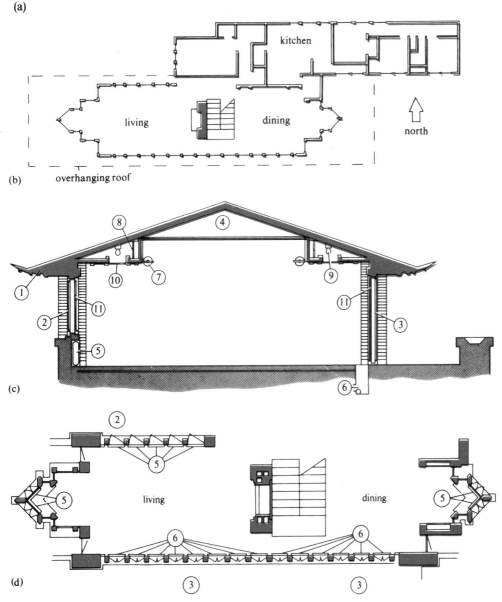

However, more recently, heating and lighting services have been liberated from the fireplace by the introduction of oil lamps and heaters, gaslight and gas fires, and most spectacularly by electric lights and heaters. And the recent introduction of 'central' heating systems has in fact created perhaps the most 'dispersed' form of heating, warmth throughout the house instead of only at the fireside.

These developments in building services of heating and lighting have had quite the opposite effect to the clustering constraints of water and waste services and the older heating and lighting services. Regions of the house remote from the fireplace can now be perfectly comfortable. Rooms can be placed where they have other advantages than mere proximity to the fireplace. The family need not spend its evenings around the kitchen stove. Activities needing good light can be performed anywhere and at any time. Perhaps most significantly a house can be 'open plan' instead of an agglomeration of box-like closed rooms.

The power-operated solutions to environmental control have led to considerable innovations in the architectural planning of houses and to significant improvements in

domestic comfort and convenience. But they do rely on the availability of power from relatively cheap fuel sources; these may not continue to be available.

In fact there has been a gradually increasing design response to the recent 'energy crises' and the awareness of finite limits to the earth's resources. This response is based on the recognition that each individual house and household cannot continue indefinitely to increase its consumption of energy and resources.

The change in approach to house design is shown diagrammatically in Figure 54. Conventionally each household has been seen as dependent on large inputs of energy and resources from mains services – electricity, water, gas, etc. – as well as food from 'mains service' producers, processors and retailers. It is almost equally dependent on being able to put out large quantities of waste, whether intentionally, as in the form of waste water and waste food, or unintentionally, as in the form of waste heat escaping through the structure. The structure itself has been seen as relatively unimportant as an insulator, since cheap fuel has been available to power environmental control through heating and air conditioning.

Figure 53   This house, designed for himself by the architect Philip Johnson in New Canaan, Connecticut, USA, in 1949, provides an example of how far the open-plan concept can be taken, given power-operated environmental control devices. Known as 'the Glass House', it is a totally glazed one-room pavilion. The interior space is undivided except for the bank of kitchen equipment and a brick cylinder housing the bathroom. A fireplace (as in the Robie house, ceremonial and psychological rather than functional) is also built into the brick cylinder. Other areas, such as for living or dining, are defined only by the location of the appropriate furniture and perhaps a floor rug, making this an ultimate open-plan house. Obviously this pavilion would be uninhabitable both in winter and summer if there were not

some other environmental controls than the single-glazed walls and flat roof. Heating is, in fact, provided over the total enclosed area by electric elements both in the floor and the ceiling. A 'passive' cooling device operates in the summer and is at first as invisible as the heating elements: it is the trees to the south and west of the house, which provide sun-shading when they are in leaf in summer (but allow the sun's rays through their leafless branches in winter). Despite this environmental subtlety, a totally single-glazed house heated by electricity is hardly an economical or energy-conserving way to keep warm, but the house was designed at a time of more profligate attitudes towards energy resources

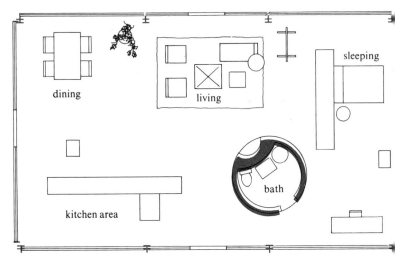

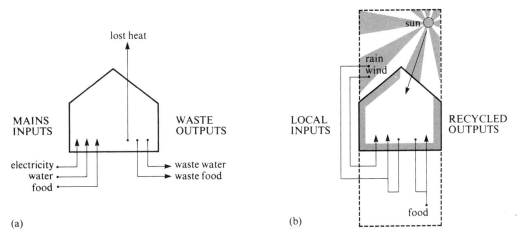

Figure 54 (a) *Old and* (b) *new models of design principles, based on a changing technological context in which energy and resources are conserved. The old model assumed large inputs from mains services and large outputs of waste. The new model utilizes small local inputs and recycles most of the outputs*

The new view of the house sees it as considerably less dependent on mains services and yet very much more dependent on its immediate environment. The result is a more autonomous house, functioning as a complete, independent system.

A first step towards 'autonomy' is to increase considerably the insulation of the house, so that it does not waste heat by leaking to the outside and so needs very little heat supplied to maintain a reasonable internal temperature. The heat supplies themselves are derived as far as possible from the immediate local environment, rather than remotely from mains services. This means trapping and using solar heat when it is available, or perhaps generating electricity by windmill, which would also be used for those few essential electrical components such as lights and pumps. Food also is grown locally and the (much reduced) wastes returned to nourish the soil as compost. Even waste water could be cleaned and re-used. A hypothetical representation of such an autonomous house is shown in Figure 55.

Figure 55 *An archetypal complete 'ecosystem' house* **Key:** *1 solar roof captures sunlight to heat water, 2 rainwater collected for home use; wind powers windmill, 3 water purified and stored, 4 decomposition of wastes produces methane gas for stove in house, 5 nutrient-rich water from treatment systems flows to fish pond and vegetable garden, 6 vegetable garden provides food, 7 animals provide food and manure*

House designs based on principles such as these can produce somewhat unfamiliar looking 'houses'. One unusual energy-conserving house, built in sunny New Mexico, USA in the early 1970s, was designed by Steve Baer (Figure 56). In this design, water-filled drums are stacked against fully glazed south-facing walls to absorb the solar heat and then gradually release it into the house at night and on sunless days. The whole-wall external insulating panels are raised to prevent loss of heat to the outside at night and on sunless days, or to control the amount of solar heat being absorbed in prolonged sunny periods. The house therefore has a high thermal capacity but with controllable solar gain and loss.

Other designs for autonomous or semi-autonomous houses may be less radical-looking, but still present rather unusual images of 'a house' (Figures 57, 58 and 59). They usually incorporate solar heat-collecting panels on the roof, have windmills attached or near by, have specific orientations and

Figure 56 The solar-heated 'zome' designed for himself by Steve Baer in Corrales, New Mexico, USA, in 1974

Figure 57 The low-energy home of Robert and Brenda Vale, near Ely, Cambridgeshire. They have converted a small nineteenth-century house to a larger but much more energy-efficient one. The conversion is based on the theoretical studies for a new 'autonomous' house, shown in Figure 58

generally require an equally unconventional life-style of their inhabitants. The designers of such houses are perhaps guilty of overemphasizing a restricted set of design factors, the environmental and technological ones, and of neglecting other factors such as socio-cultural ones.

However, these radical designs do show, by contrast, just how much conventional houses (and the life-styles within them) are dependent on the 'invisible' back-up of technological services.

Figure 58 A design for an 'autonomous' house by Brenda Vale, at Cambridge University Department of Architecture. (a) View from south-east; (b) plans; (c) section. The single-storey house has a solar-collector roof and a fully glazed conservatory facing south. All the other walls are heavily insulated. Warm air, heated by the sun in the conservatory, is pumped into the living rooms. Underfloor storage heaters of sand and earth are heated similarly and by hot water from the solar collector and electricity from the windmill

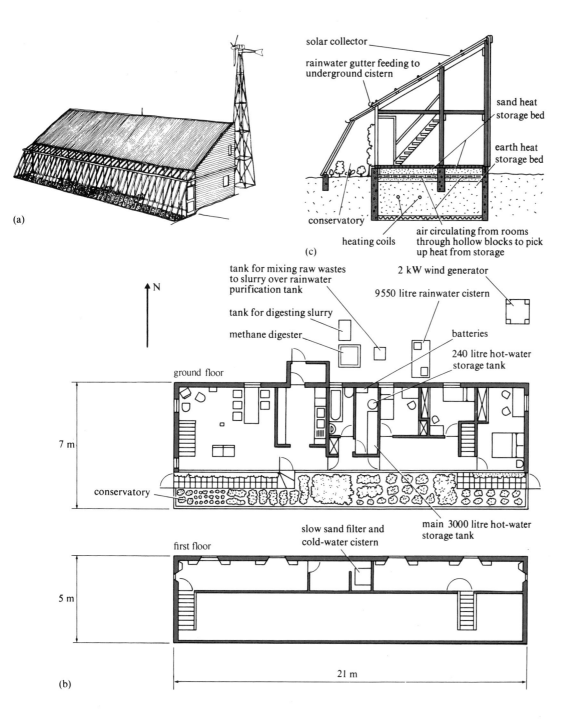

(a)

solar collector

rainwater gutter feeding to underground cistern

sand heat storage bed

earth heat storage bed

conservatory

heating coils

air circulating from rooms through hollow blocks to pick up heat from storage

(c)

tank for mixing raw wastes to slurry over rainwater purification tank

2 kW wind generator

9550 litre rainwater cistern

tank for digesting slurry

methane digester

batteries

240 litre hot-water storage tank

ground floor

N

7 m

conservatory

slow sand filter and cold-water cistern

main 3000 litre hot-water storage tank

first floor

5 m

21 m

(b)

Summary

A house can be designed as an essentially passive construction for modifying the local climate, collecting or reflecting solar heat etc., but in cold and temperate climates it is usually necessary to add active forms of environmental control, such as heating. This and the many other forms of building services in a modern house have a significant influence on house design. Usually it is necessary to plan the house so that similar services are adjacent. Twentieth-century developments in domestic services, such as central heating, have offered greater design freedom, such as the possibility of open-plan houses. However, if there is a shortage of, or desire to conserve, energy and other resources, houses may have to be designed in radically different ways so as to make them less dependent on mains services.

(a)

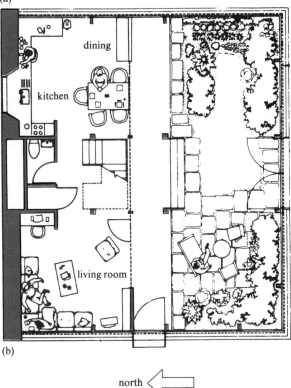

(b)

north

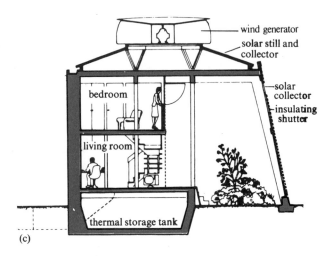

Figure 59   A design by Alexander Pike, also at the Cambridge University Department of Architecture. This is a two-storey house, half of which is a large greenhouse. The rest of the space can be continuous with the greenhouse or closed off with insulating shutters. The realistic photograph (a) is, in fact, only of a model; (b) is the plan and (c) a section

64

(c)

Activity 5   Services

The purpose of this activity is to assess how the service installations may have influenced the plan of your house. (Estimated activity time: about $\frac{1}{2}$–1 hour.)

Draw a plan of your house so that the service installations and the service spaces (bathroom, lavatory, circulation spaces) are emphasized; for example, use heavy lines and different colours for different services. Try to make the services 'stand out' from the plan as clearly as possible. This is a model of your house seen from a 'service' viewpoint. What do you notice about the locations of the various services relative to each other? How efficiently planned are the service spaces? Consider whether the lengths of piping etc. have been efficiently minimized. Consider also whether the planning for the services has seriously affected your freedom in the way you might like to use your house.

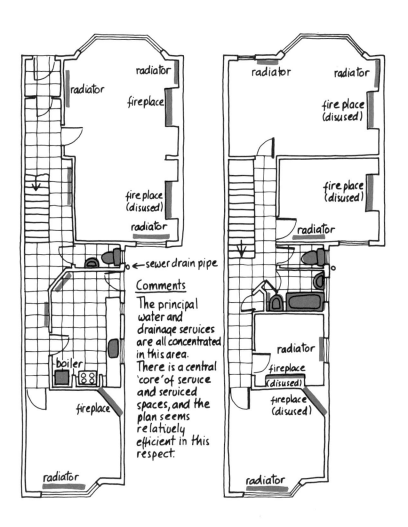

10　As safe as houses

At one time it was quite common for houses of the poorer people (i.e. the majority) in Britain to be so badly constructed that they suffered extensive damage, even total collapse, in gales. There is still a strong feeling against the inadequate constructional standards of 'jerry-builders'. In this section we shall be concerned with just one aspect of constructional efficiency, that of structural stability, and its influence in the design of a house.

Nowadays houses tend to be very stable, except for the occasional catastrophe such as the collapse of the Ronan Point flats in London in 1968 (Figure 60). In fact they are usually much more stable than they ever need to be in the face of the strongest gales; they could bend, sag or sway much more than they do without necessarily being structurally unsafe. This structural 'over-design' (i.e. making the structure much stronger and stiffer than it theoretically needs to be) does, however, have some compensations, not the least of which is its contribution to the peace of mind of the house's occupants; people simply don't *feel* safe in a house that bends and sways.

The human body is very sensitive to sensations of vibration, and if you feel a building vibrating apparently quite strongly it is probably in fact only moving the minutest amounts. Buildings can, nevertheless, literally shake in the wind, although without necessarily being structurally unsafe. The Empire State Building in New York, for instance, sways as much as 60 cm (2 feet) at its tip, but is not in any danger of collapse.

The Empire State Building has a steel frame structural 'skeleton' that can cope with the building's swaying in the wind. If it were simply built of bricks or stone, then you could imagine that it would not be at all safe. Thin, straight, brick or stone walls built to such a height would not be able to resist the inevitable swaying and twisting and would certainly collapse. If you want to pile unreinforced bricks or stones to a great height, then you have to adopt a very different basic shape for the building, say like the ancient pyramids of Egypt.

This suggests that certain materials lend themselves more naturally to certain building forms than others, as you saw in the examples of vernacular houses in Part One, where the various house shapes are partly determined by the structural possibilities of the materials from which they are made. You are probably familiar with the idea of the

Figure 60　One corner of the Ronan Point flats in London collapsed in 1968. The flats were 'system-built' of large panels and a gas explosion on one of the upper floors blew out one of the panels

relation between materials and the kinds of structural forms to which they lend themselves from your own experience (like that of the vernacular house builders) of building simple structures from readily available on-site materials. If, for a moment, you have forgotten about this personal building experience, I should remind you that I am thinking of the experiences I am sure you have had in building such things as sandcastles, and perhaps also mud 'pies' and snowmen.

What can you recall from your experiences of building sandcastles that suggests something of the relationship between material properties and structural forms?

My own recollections of building sandcastles are:

1   It is very difficult to build anything except simple mounds with *dry* sand. It has to be dampened in order to make the grains of sand stick together.

2   Even damp sand has to be built in rounded, mounded shapes; vertical walls and sharp corners soon slip and crumble into more natural forms.

3   It is very difficult to make large openings in a sandcastle wall. The wall above simply collapses into the opening. All the openings have to be arched at their tops.

rounded, mounded shapes

small arched openings

Figure 61   Basic structural features of sandcastles

Other kinds of material have quite different structural properties and lend themselves naturally to quite different structural forms. You have probably had some experience of building with timber, for example, even if it is only to make some bookshelves from timber planks. Unlike sand and earth, timber can usefully span quite large openings, supporting the load (e.g. the books) above, even if it sometimes sags visibly under the load.

One other material with which you may have had some building experience is canvas, used in a tent. This kind of material has completely different qualities again from that of timber or earth. On its own it is virtually useless as a shelter; it has to be supported by other materials, the tent poles or frame of timber or metal. However, providing that it is

kept taut, it can span quite large areas without intermediate support.

The materials that occur naturally, without too much reworking or re-forming by people (i.e. excluding materials such as plastics and metals) are from three sources: the earth itself, vegetation and animal skins. Earth-based materials include mud, stone and brick; these all tend towards massive structural forms with small openings, and the volume of space they can enclose is often determined by the skill of the builder in making vaults and domes. (Remember the example of Durham cathedral in the *Introduction*, as well as the *trulli* and Pueblo and Dogon houses in Part One?) Materials from vegetable sources include timber, thatch, bamboo and grass; these offer possibilities of much lighter open structures, with flat or sloping roofs spanning relatively large areas. Animal-skin materials include hides and also sheet materials made from animal wool or hair; these need other materials to provide supports, but can span moderate areas, and lead to structural forms that are peaked and angular – the classic tent form.

The different materials lend themselves to different basic structural forms because of the kinds of forces they are able to bear. Earth-based materials are granular and tend to crumble apart when pulled (i.e. under forces of *tension*), but are good at resisting forces that tend to *compress* them. Sheet materials on the other hand (whether hides or woven from wool or from vegetable materials) have no compressive resistance and won't stand up, even under just their own weight, but they are usually good in tension, to provide a taut awning, for example. Timber, bamboo, and some other vegetable-based materials have properties that enable them to resist forces of both tension and compression, and so to span openings and to play a versatile structural role.

So, from a structural point of view, the design of any building is a matter of matching the available materials to suitable structural forms. The *trulli*, for example, have conical roofs, which are a form that it is possible (with skill) to construct from small stones. The tepee is another cone, but made by leaning timber supports together and draping them with skins. An igloo is a hemispherical dome, which it is possible to construct of snow. And so on.

Of course, the resulting structure also has to be strong enough to cope with the loads it has to carry. Building a dome out of stones might be a suitable match of form and materials, but the dome might still collapse if it is not thick enough to carry the external loads imposed on it by wind, snow, or whatever, as well as carrying its own weight. Therefore the material has to be used in sizes and thicknesses that are appropriate to its inherent strength.

Clearly, some materials are stronger than others. You would rightly guess that a steel hawser is much stronger than a normal hemp rope of the same size. But not all comparisons are so obvious. If you could imagine a rope made of spider's web, for example, would you expect it to be stronger or weaker than a hemp rope of the same size? Although it is not practically possible to make a rope of spider's web, in theory it would be about three times as strong as a hemp rope.

Questions such as 'How strong is a piece of rope?' are rather like the proverbial 'How long is a piece of string?' It all depends on the piece in question, of course. But every material does have an inherent strength, which can be measured, and which is known as the maximum *stress* the material can withstand before breaking. A steel hawser can withstand a much higher stress than a hemp rope of the same thickness, but you might be able to find a rope that can carry the same maximum *load* as the hawser; it would have to be much thicker, though.

The mechanical properties of materials, such as the stress they can withstand, govern their usefulness as load-bearing parts of a building. For example, you would not expect to find stone beams being used for the rafters in the roof of a house. These mechanical properties (and others) also influence the *types* of structures that can be made – tall buildings, large domes, long bridges, and so on. The scale and complexity of modern buildings and other structures have been made possible by an increased understanding of how structures in general, and the materials from which they are made, respond to the loads imposed on them. Some of the basic principles of this understanding are introduced in the *Structures and Materials* tributary.

You know that if you have some timber bookshelves that are sagging under their load and threatening to break, you can either replace them with ones of another, stiffer material, or with thicker ones. What other ways might you reduce the sag in a bookshelf? You could do it either by reducing the load (taking some of the books off) or by reducing the span of the shelf, that is, by reducing the distance between its supports (perhaps by adding another shelf bracket between the original ones).

Unfortunately, thicker shelves are more expensive than thinner ones, so you would probably want to use the thinnest ones you could that did not sag in an unseemly fashion over the distance between the supports you have provided for them. There is a fairly clear relationship between thickness and span: the wider the span, then the thicker must be the shelf. You would probably want to make a reasonable trade-off between the thickness of the shelf and the number of brackets you have to provide to support it.

The situation is very similar in the general structural design of your whole house. If all the walls were very close together then the spans of the floors and roof would be very small, and they could be made of very slight, inexpensive material. However, a lot of supporting walls would in themselves be expensive as well as very inconveniently dividing the house into a lot of very small rooms. Conversely, if the walls were very far apart then the floors and roof would have to be made much stronger to span the space between the walls. The builder therefore tries to strike something near a satisfactory compromise arrangement in which the walls are as near together as is both convenient and economic. Normally there are more walls than is structurally necessary, anyway, since each room has four walls, yet its floor and ceiling span between only two of them. In a rectangular room, therefore, the floor and ceiling usually span across the shorter dimension.

The essential feature of any building structure is that it encloses space, that is, it creates an enveloped volume within which the climate can be modified, people can conveniently carry on their domestic activities and so on. Therefore the structural properties of materials are important in creating a variety of possibilities for the enclosure of space, and because they limit the kinds of spaces that can be created with certain materials.

What kinds of spaces – what shapes, areas, volumes, etc. – do people want to provide for themselves? Obviously this is determined by many factors, including the customs and traditions of different cultures. In Western 'functional' culture people look for efficient ways of enclosing space; this leads to some structural forms being preferred over others.

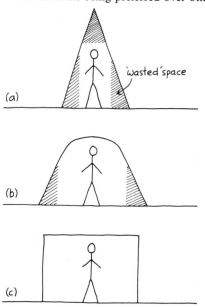

Figure 62 Efficiency of space utilization in different basic structural forms of enclosure; (a) ridged 'tent' form, (b) domed form, (c) rectangular form

If you have lived even for a short time in a ridge-tent, you will have realized some of the deficiencies of that form of space enclosure. In cross-section its narrow peaked form provides only a small central space where the headroom may be enough for a standing person. Outside this central area the enclosed space is less useful or even 'wasted', except for storage (Figure 62).

Notice again how clearly a point can be made, or reinforced, by using simple diagrams (Figure 62).

What is needed, then, is to enclose a wider space more efficiently. A vault or dome goes some way towards achieving this, although it still leaves some 'waste' space.

It becomes clear that what is necessary is a structural form that approximates to a rectangular space enclosure. Such a form requires some width of span to provide convenience and economy of enclosure. This is the structural and spatial form of the conventional Western European house, with vertical walls of brick, stone or timber frame, spanned by a timber superstructure to carry the sloping roof necessary to shed the rainwater. Its cross-section (Figure 63) has become the very symbol for 'house' in Western European culture.

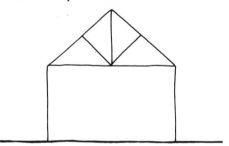

Figure 63   Conventional Western European house structure

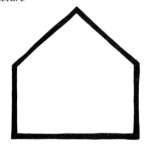

Figure 64   Symbol for 'house' in Western European culture

To a large degree this conventional Western house form arose from the use of timber as the principal structural material. Timber is such a useful and versatile building material that it has been used as a major component in shelters from earliest times, both as a structural component and for cladding and enclosing open frameworks. Wood has particular properties that account

for its suitability as a building material. It resists both tensile and compressive structural forces, and can span reasonable distances. It is relatively light and therefore easily manipulated in the constructional process.

It can be easily worked with simple tools, to shape it and to construct joints between separate members. It is warm to the touch and has some moderately good thermal insulating characteristics. Finally, timber is widely available, since trees grow over wide areas of the earth's land surface.

Exercise

You have just read a clear, but succinct, paragraph on the properties of wood. This is the sort of topic on which you should be keeping notes. In your notebook, try making your own notes on the properties of wood, first in a linear form, and then in a spray diagram.

Discussion

Wood:

resists tensile and compressive structural forces;

spans distances;

is light and so is easily manipulated when building;

is easily worked with simple tools;

feels warm;

is a reasonable thermal insulator.

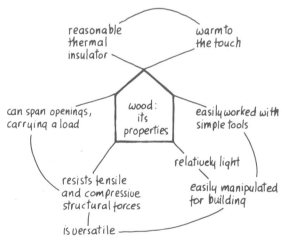

As usual, your own interpretation and links in the diagram may be different. The technical terms (e.g. 'tensile', 'compressive') have been used because they save space. But it is important to define them for yourself in your study notebook, based on what you learn from *Structures and Materials*.

Timber houses still predominate in some countries of the world, particularly where the timber forests have not been depleted, for

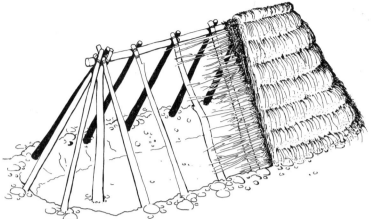

Figure 65   A simple Anglo-Saxon shelter

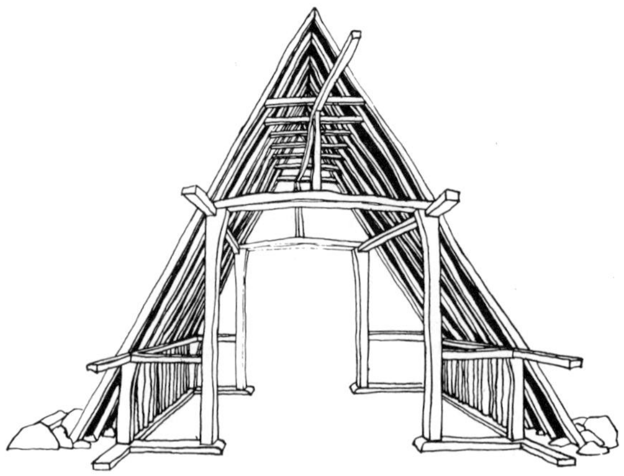

Figure 66   Example of an early 'notched' frame. Only when iron tools became available was it possible to cut and fit together accurate timber frames

instance, in the northern European countries and in some of the northern states of the USA. In Britain timber houses were once common, but became more rare as the forests dwindled.

Some of the earliest timber shelters would have been little more than thatched tent-like structures (Figure 65), open at one end and rounded at the other. A ridge pole supported the lean-to wall/roof members, which were secured at their bases by stones and perhaps a small earth bank. Obviously the usable living space (as in a ridge tent) is limited, and the only way to increase it in this structural form is to use very long wall/roof members, supported against sagging by horizontal beams (called purlins), as in early examples of a 'notched frame' (Figure 66).

To increase the usable living space further, without using extraordinarily long (and perhaps unobtainable) wall/roof timbers, either some vertical wall elements or else a form of vaulting had to be introduced. The latter is in fact what happened in the kind of timber frame found quite often in Britain and known as a cruck frame. A cruck is formed by a pair of shaped timbers forming an arch (Figure 67). Such shaped timbers could be found in suitably bent trees or boughs and by splitting such a tree or bough longitudinally a matching pair of timbers could be made.

The other line of development was into a box-frame form of construction (Figure 68), which, of course, has continued with refinements into conventional present-day timber frames. Cruck construction itself continued in Britain well into the nineteenth century, developing its own refinements.

The most significant structural developments were in the gradual sophistication of forms of roof frameworks, such as trusses, to span greater widths (Figure 69). This sophistication became possible as the structural properties of timber became known with more certainty and as the behaviour of structural forces in a frame or truss became known.

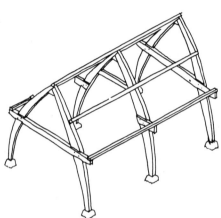

Figure 67   A cruck frame, using naturally shaped timbers

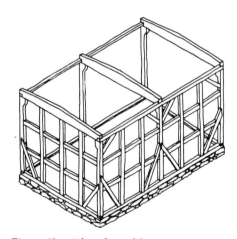

Figure 68   A box-framed house structure

This would be a good point to break off to study *Structures and Materials*. Sections 1 and 2 consider some of the mechanical properties of materials and how structures behave under load. Section 3 is concerned with the problem of bridging the gap between the walls of a building, and with roof structures.

Summary

Particular materials lend themselves more 'naturally' to certain structural shapes and forms because of the kinds of forces they can carry, whether tensile or compressive forces. Different materials also have different strengths measured by the stress they can withstand. To carry a certain load over a certain span, the material used must be of an appropriate thickness. If the span is increased, then the thickness of the structural member must be increased and so there is a trade-off to be made between the number of supports and the thickness of the member. The basic structural design problem is one of enclosing a convenient space efficiently and economically. An important development has been the gradual refinement of the triangular timber roof truss; in fact a familiar symbol for 'house' in Western culture is based on the conventional triangular-roofed, straight-sided structural form.

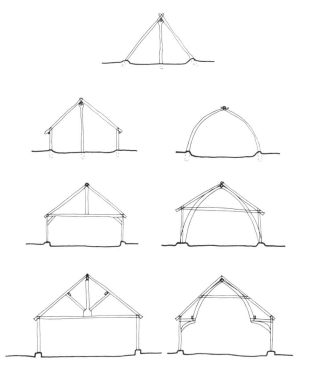

Figure 69   The development and refinement of box frames with triangular roof trusses (left) and of cruck frames (right)

Figure 70   New structural design possibilities in the twentieth century have created some dramatic architectural concepts. The 'Kaufman house' (also known as 'Falling Water') at Bear Run, Pennsylvania, USA, was designed by Frank Lloyd Wright in 1936. He used reinforced concrete to create cantilevered balconies and terraces over a dramatic natural setting of rocks, pools and waterfalls

Figure 71   The 'Farnsworth house' at Plano, Illinois, USA, designed by Mies van der Rohe in 1946, is a more discrete 'statement' of the house's structure, in this case a steel frame. The floor of the house is raised above the ground because of the annual springtime floods of a nearby river, but this also provides an excuse for the neat structural frame to be shown off. The interior open-planning is very similar to the Philip Johnson 'Glass House' (Figure 53)

Activity 6   Structure

The purpose of this activity is to help you to analyse and understand the major structural organization of your house. (Estimated activity time: about $\frac{1}{2}$–1 hour.)

1   Draw a plan of your house as seen from above, a roof plan. Show the lines of the ridges and valleys of the roof, that is, the places where the slope of the roof changes. You will probably have to go outside and get the best view of your roof that you can in order to get this right. If you have a flat roof this activity is unfortunately irrelevant to you in terms of what you can learn about your roof structure.

2   Draw onto the roof plan double-headed arrows showing the lines of slope of the major roof areas. These arrows indicate the directions of span of the rafters inside the roof. You can now identify which are the major load-bearing walls (or sections of wall) that carry the weight of the roof. The principal rafters bear at their ends onto these load-bearing walls. Using a thick marker, clearly show these load-bearing walls, so that you have a graphic representation of which walls are carrying the major roof loads.

3   If you have a two-storey house, the other major structural problem in its construction would have been the spanning of the first floor. These floors are usually of timber floorboards nailed to timber beams (joists) that span between the walls. The floorboards are laid across the joists and so the direction they run is at right angles to the direction of span of the joists. From observing your first-floor floorboards, therefore, you can tell which way the joists span beneath them. If you have a fairly modern house, you may have large sheets of chipboard laid instead of the more familiar narrow floorboards, but you should still be able to see how the joists run underneath, from the positions of the lines of nail-heads showing where the boards have been fixed to the joists below.

4   Draw a *ground*-floor plan of your house, with double-headed arrows superimposed, showing the directions of span of the joists *above*. Again, these arrows will point to the major load-bearing walls, but this time to those walls that carry the first-floor load. Mark these load-bearing sections to show graphically your understanding of the distribution of the first-floor load.

5   Combine your two plans (roof plan and ground floor) into one at ground-floor level, clearly showing all the major load-bearing wall sections. Include those walls that must carry the roof loads through to the ground, as well as those carrying the first-floor load.

(NB. Do not go knocking holes in walls you think you have identified as non-load-bearing without first getting specialist advice to confirm your analysis.)

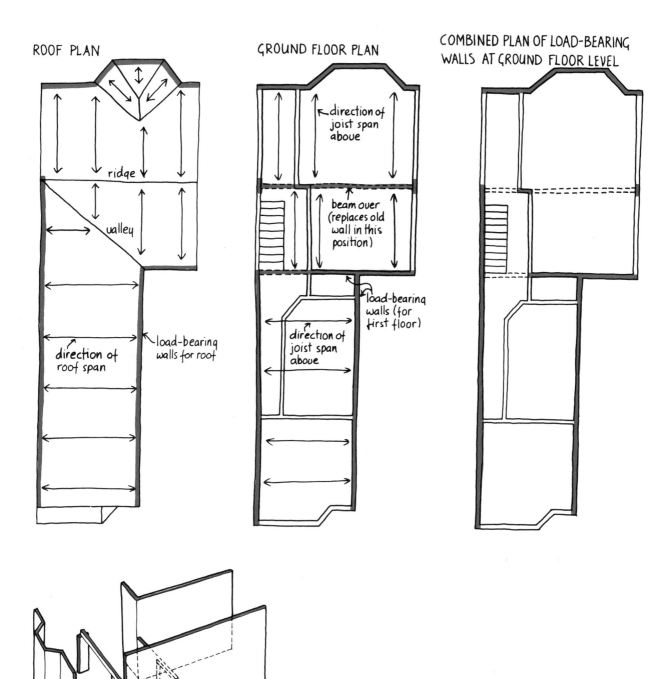

ROOF PLAN

ridge

valley

direction of
roof span

load-bearing
walls for roof

GROUND FLOOR PLAN

direction of
joist span
above

beam over
(replaces old
wall in this
position)

load-bearing
walls (for
first floor)

direction of
joist span
above

COMBINED PLAN OF LOAD-BEARING
WALLS AT GROUND FLOOR LEVEL

The principal load-bearing walls of my house

Part Three   Design

11   The story so far

At this point let me recap what you have learnt so far, before you start on this final part of Block 1 *Home*.

In the diagram at the end of Part One (Figure 13) I tried to show how, in the design of a house, there is a necessary integration of two major sets of factors: human requirements on the one hand and technical capabilities on the other. I have repeated the diagram here (Figure 72) and you should now be able to understand much more fully and clearly what I meant by it.

Firstly, you should understand why people 'need' a house. For instance, you have learnt about the standards people normally require for thermal comfort, about the supply of heat to meet these standards, and how house design (in terms of shape, orientation, and use of building materials) can influence, and be influenced by, heating requirements. You have learnt also about spatial standards and the arrangement of rooms to meet Western ideas of convenience. In general, all of these needs have been set in a context of the social and cultural factors that are usually inseparable from any considerations of the plan, the overall form or the appearance of a house.

Secondly, you should understand something of how technology 'provides' a house. You have learnt some of the basic properties of materials that relate to their use in a house, such as their strengths, their structural capabilities and their thermal properties. You have learnt of the influence of building services in house design and of the influence of structural mechanics.

Throughout your study of Part Two you were also learning to 'see' your own house from different points of view. This ability, to be able to 'see' situations from different points of view, is one of the central aspects of thinking in terms of 'systems'. As explained in the *Introduction*, a *system* is a mental construct used to understand something or some situation better. The system has a *boundary* and within that boundary there is a richly connected assembly of components which operate together. Each different view of a house has effectively defined a slightly

different 'system'. For example, in Part One we were considering a 'cultural system for providing shelter' and noticed how differences in climate, available materials and culture produced a wide range of 'houses'. In Section 7 we were effectively regarding the house as 'an arrangement of spaces for carrying out a range of activities'. In Section 8 the house became 'a system for providing thermal comfort' and in Section 10 it was a structural system, one that had to withstand environmental forces and the activities of the occupants.

Expressing these different 'views' of the house in terms of systems helps to formalize the differences implicit in each view. Going through the process of actually identifying the boundary of each system is a very good way of thinking through the consistency of each view. It is also a very useful first step for *modelling* that particular system. For example, in considering the house as 'an arrangement of spaces for carrying out a range of activities' it is not immediately obvious where to draw the boundary. The earlier discussions restricted the system to being within the physical boundary of the house structure, but for some activities it would be appropriate to include any garden or garage or access paths. Similarly, when considering the house as 'a system for providing thermal comfort' it is not clear whether the boundary should be drawn around the physical home. Should it

Figure 72   Conceptual diagram of the block

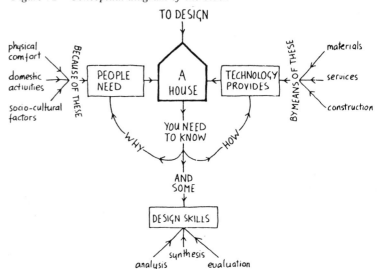

also include nearby trees and houses, which will affect the solar gains and exposure to the wind? And should it also include some or all of the systems used to deliver fuels to the home? There is no 'right' choice of system boundary in cases like this; each choice will reflect a particular 'view' of the situation, will require a different model and will elucidate different aspects of the total situation. For instance, if we wish to compare the effects of using different heating fuels in a house we get a different perspective by drawing a boundary around the perimeter of the house than if we had included the fuel systems as well. In all these cases the formalism of identifying the system and carefully defining the boundary provides pay-offs in terms of clearer thinking and, usually, better modelling.

In the activities associated with each 'view' or system you were introduced to an appropriate *model* of that aspect of the house. I deliberately elected to use fairly simple models because I wanted you to appreciate the range of models that could be brought to bear on something like a house. I also happen to believe that it is essential to start with simple models since, if well constructed, these will elucidate the main relationships involved and provide the necessary groundwork for moving on to more sophisticated models.

Besides giving you practice in modelling skills, the activities had two other important purposes. One was to affect your attitude to your house, so that you would become constructively critical of it; not only of how it *is*, but also of how it *might be* designed or redesigned. As the rest of this course develops, this critical attitude should extend through and beyond the particular, perhaps rather trivial, example of your own house to technology in general.

The other important purpose of the activities was to enable you to see that many different factors have to be combined in order to make a successful design solution. If one, or just a few, of the many factors is emphasized at the expense of the others, then it can only result in a partial design solution rather than a whole one. This is true of great works of architecture, engineering and design, just as it is true of a modest conventional house such as yours and mine.

The above considerations must also be true of unconventional houses such as the 'dome home' shown in Figure 73. The house consists of a hemispherical dome, about 10 metres in diameter, made of pressed steel segmental sections lined internally with polyurethane foam insulation. The internal environment is maintained almost invariably at about 20 °C despite the extreme external winter and summer temperatures which can range from −20 °C to 40 °C on that particular site in New Mexico. Heating is provided by hot water circulating from a heavily insulated external storage tank, the water being heated from the sun by means of solar collector panels. Electricity is provided from windmills. The house is therefore 100% self-sufficient in energy terms.

To achieve that energy self-sufficiency, one of the design decisions made by the designer was to use a domed shape since that gave a maximum enclosed space for minimum external surface area. But that, you might think, was a failure on the 'needs' side of the diagram, because it doesn't necessarily lead to a convenient arrangement of interior spaces. It certainly fails in meeting the usual social and cultural visual standards, too, since it really doesn't *look* like a home. However, on the 'provisions' side of the diagram, you should be able to understand how materials, construction, and services have been combined successfully to meet the radical requirement of energy self-sufficiency.

In Part Two you were learning to *analyse* and to *evaluate* existing design solutions. Now, you must turn your attention to that other, central aspect of design skill: you must learn to *synthesize*, or create, new design solutions of your own.

It is often said that any design has to be a *compromise* between many *conflicting* factors. Having analysed and evaluated your own house, you may feel this is a realistic view of the difficult task of designing. However, I think that a good designer, rather than being willing to accept the shortcomings of a compromise, should aim to create a *synthesis* of the many *complementary* factors in any design problem and its solution. In other words, the design should try to find a form of solution in which all the factors work together rather than pulling against each other.

As you can realize, creating this kind of synthesis is not always (if ever) easy. It is the challenge that awaits you in the next section!

Figure 73
Robert Reines' 'dome home'

12 Design task

To complete the calculations involved in the design task described in this section, you need to be familiar with how to use your computer, how to use the computer program Framework and how to use spreadsheets. You therefore need to have completed your study of Block 1 *Computing* before attempting the design task.

Introduction

The task that forms Part Three of Block 1 *Home* and is the basis of the tutor-marked assignment involves designing a small single-storey house. In order to make this job manageable within the time you have available, and in order to make it possible for you to carry out some calculations – of cost and heat loss – in relation to your design, a considerable number of constraints have been imposed on the problem. These constraints impose rather severe limits on your freedom in design. They also serve to make the process of designing, and the finished product itself, slightly artificial and unrealistic.

I hope, however, that you can accept these unavoidable limitations in return for what I believe the experience of going through the exercise *can* provide. By doing this exercise you should gain some insight into the nature of the designer's job and methods of work, and some understanding of the interaction of many aspects of the technology of building, and how these have to be reconciled in the finally selected design. Thus many of the features of house design that you have been looking at *analytically* in Part Two must now be brought together in the *synthetic* process of design.

Briefly, what you are going to be asked to do is to arrange a given number of rooms in a plan so that certain functional relations between the rooms are satisfied. You will then need to decide on the details of construction of the house, taking account of some structural considerations. The components of construction (doors, windows, sections of wall and roof, etc.) are of given sizes, costs and physical properties. It is as though the house were made from a kit of prefabricated parts. You will be able to set out each of your designs on a gridded sheet representing the site, by sticking down adhesive strips of different colours. Within each room you can arrange furniture and fittings, by tracing the plan views of these items from the printed card supplied.

Then for each plan you have to carry out, with the help of your computer, calculations on the costs of constructing and heating this building. The design aim is to minimize the annual running costs of the house. For the purpose of this exercise the running costs are the mortgage repayments and the heating bills. You will carry out the calculations using a set of prepared spreadsheets for use in Framework.

> The precise form of the tutor-marked assignment will change from year to year. You should consult the notes on the assignments for Block 1 for details of what should be submitted and information on how your work will be assessed. Generally you will be asked to submit the following items:
>
> A series of house plans represented on the gridded 'site plans'.
>
> Corresponding to each plan, a summary of the insulation, heating, building and total annual costs.
>
> Most important, a written account *in note form* of the various decisions that you have made in the course of the design process. (The study notes included in previous parts of the mainstream should be helpful to you here.) You will need to explain the reasoning that has gone into each particular plan, and to set down the results of the various critical assessments and evaluations made of that plan.

You should therefore now check that you have to hand the following 'equipment' (as supplied in the Design Task envelope):

gridded site plans;

adhesive strips and labels to represent components of construction;

printed card showing plan views of furniture and fittings.

Also you may need some card or stiff paper and scissors, in order to cut out shapes to represent the rooms when you are arranging the plan.

It follows from what I have said so far, that the process of design that you will go through will involve two distinct stages: stages that are typical of the design process in general and not just of architectural design. The first stage involves manipulating a set of *components* (in this case rooms and constructional components) in order to produce spatial arrangements or designs, within the limits set by certain functional (or aesthetic) *constraints*. We might call this the *generative* or *compositional* part of the design process, in which alternative arrangements are generated or put together.

In the second stage these designs are subjected to tests, or to criticisms, of various kinds. This we might call the *evaluative* part of the process. In this exercise the evaluative part of the process involves the calculation of construction and heating costs. For any one design you will be able to find the level of insulation that minimizes the annual costs. By examining the contributions to the calculations you may also be able to see ways to change the overall design to improve its performance. You may also like to make evaluations of a qualitative, less formal nature; for example, you could imagine how the rooms will be used, what the house will look like and how the lighting in the room might appear.

As a result of such evaluations or tests you may decide to choose some designs rather than others, and you may wish to make some changes to those designs in order to improve their performance in certain respects. These new revised designs can be evaluated once more, and so the cycle goes on – of repeated alternating phases of 'generation' and 'evaluation' – until you are satisfied with the result (or run out of time).

All this is by way of explanation as to why the various limitations, some of which may seem arbitrary to you, have been placed on your freedom in the 'generative' part of the process. If you were free to choose whatever materials you liked, whatever geometrical forms you wanted, whatever structural arrangement you wished, then it would be very difficult indeed for you to proceed to the 'evaluative' stage. You might be able to 'compose' a most imaginative and original plan, but you would not be able to work out how much it would cost, whether it would be difficult to heat, say, or whether it would be structurally sound, since you would not be able to apply the necessarily limited techniques of calculation that you have learnt so far. What is more, it would be virtually impossible, in the space of this short text, to supply you with sufficient information, about costs, about building materials, about structural systems, to answer all the questions that would arise if your choice in design was completely unrestricted.

It is very important that you should get right through the process of design to the point where you can make precise quantitative evaluations, by means of detailed calculations of cost and performance. It is only by doing this, by going round the cycle of 'generate and test' a number of times, that you will really gain some insights into the interrelations of the various factors involved and how conflicting requirements might be reconciled or resolved.

The exercise, then, is highly simplified by comparison with what an architect does in practice; however, it is not lacking in realism. The heating and cost calculations carried out in the spreadsheets are actually more sophisticated than those normally carried out by an architect (though of course the costs used in the spreadsheet apply only to the year – 1988 – when the spreadsheet was assembled). The way in which different aspects of the arrangement, materials and performance of the design are interrelated and affect one another is broadly indicative of these same factors in real buildings. At the end of the exercise you will have the opportunity of criticizing and changing the 'rules' that have been imposed, and of widening the range of choices available in the design of an 'ideal' house, with yourself as client.

The overall geometry of the house

Suppose for the moment that the site for the house is flat and that there are no neighbouring buildings, trees or other obstructions anywhere close by. This will be relevant when we come to consider sunshine falling on the windows of the house. The plan of the house is to be laid out on a square grid, whose lines are spaced one metre apart. It is quite usual to employ a grid of this kind in architectural design, because it facilitates the fitting together of factory-made components in standard sizes. This standardization is known as 'modular co-ordination'. In houses it would be unusual to have such a large module, however; a unit of 300 mm would be more normal. Indeed almost *all* modern houses are effectively designed on some kind of modular grid. For instance in brick construction most plan dimensions will tend to be some multiple of 114 mm (4½ inches), which is the length of a half-brick; and in wooden construction the standard sizes of timber members or sheet materials will often determine the module.

You are asked in your design, therefore, to place all walls, windows and doors along these lines and thus confine yourself to a generally rectangular geometry. The scale of the grid representing the site plan is 1:50, so that each 20 mm square on the paper corresponds to one metre actual size. The roof of the house is to be flat, for the sake of structural simplicity, and the height of the building, from floor to roof level, is 2.5 metres.

The rooms

The plan is to comprise five separate rooms: a living room, a kitchen/diner, two bedrooms and a bathroom. In addition, you may wish to have a separate circulation space, a hall or corridor, although this is optional. The rooms are each to be of simple rectangular shape and they are to be separate enclosed spaces with doors; you must suppose that the clients for the house do not want any open-plan type of arrangement.

There are certain limits on the sizes of the rooms. Each one must not be smaller in floor area than a certain size, because it would not be possible to provide the required space for activities and furniture in less area, and it must not be larger than a specified area, for reasons of cost.

There is an additional constraint imposed on the shapes of rooms. I have already said that they must be rectangular, but these rectangles must not be made too thin and long, since this would make them inconvenient or even unusable. The limit set is that the length of the longer side must not be greater than twice the shorter side.

Upper and lower limits are set on the areas of rooms as follows:

Bathroom: not less than $4\,m^2$; not more than $6\,m^2$.

Kitchen/diner: not less than $12\,m^2$; not more than $16\,m^2$.

Bedroom 1: not less than $12\,m^2$; not more than $16\,m^2$.

Bedroom 2: not less than $8\,m^2$; not more than $12\,m^2$.

Living room: not less than $15\,m^2$; not more than $18\,m^2$.

For the hall or corridor there are no limitations on size or shape, other than the fact that walls must lie on the 1 m grid. Thus the effective minimum width for a corridor is one metre.

Now all these combined limits on size and shape, together with the constraints imposed by the grid, allow only very few alternatives for each room. I have chosen the dimensions in such a way that the rooms are all of a size and shape that is appropriate to their functions (although at the lower limits they are rather small). It is possible to fit in suitable furniture and equipment of standard sizes and types; later on you will have the opportunity to do this. It may be that you will prefer certain of the allowed sizes because of particular pieces of furniture or features of room layout that you want to include.

At this stage, however, I suggest that you work out what *all* the possibilities are within the limits set; since the knowledge of the available shapes and sizes will help at the next step in the process, when you come to assemble the plan as a whole. You should find that there are only two possibilities of size and shape for the bathroom and three each for the kitchen/diner, living room and bedrooms.

Functional relations between the rooms

You can now proceed to the problem of putting the given rooms together in a plan so that certain required functional relations between them are satisfied. You will go through a process therefore which is effectively the reverse of the exercise that you previously went through with your own house, analysing its plan to determine the relations existing between rooms. Remember that, in that exercise, you drew a functional diagram in which the rooms were represented by circles and, wherever two rooms were immediately connected by a door, this was shown on the diagram by a line between the two circles. Here a similar notation will be used to show the relations that must be satisfied in the plan you design. You will see later on that the width of a door is to be 1 metre. So, if two rooms are placed so as to overlap by only one unit on the 1 metre grid, this will be sufficient to allow for the interconnecting doorway (Figure 74).

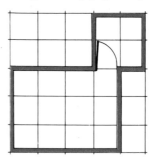

Figure 74 Minimum overlap between rooms to allow for a door is 1 metre

The required functional relations are:

(a) There should be direct access from the outside to the kitchen/diner.

(b) If there is no separate circulation space, there should be direct access from the living room to the kitchen/diner. If there is a separate circulation space, then access between kitchen/diner and living room can be via the circulation (and there is no necessity for direct access from the living room to the kitchen).

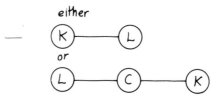

(c) If there is no separate circulation space, there should be direct access from the outside to the living room. But if there is a separate circulation space, there should be direct access from the outside to the circulation, and from the circulation to the living room (and there is no necessary requirement for direct access from the outside to the living room).

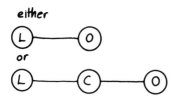

(d) Similarly, if there is no separate circulation space, there should be direct access from the bedrooms to the bathroom. But if there is separate circulation, there should be direct access from the bedrooms to the circulation and from the circulation to the bathroom (and there is no necessity for direct access from the bathroom to the bedrooms).

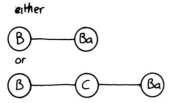

(e) Similarly, if there is no separate circulation space, there should be direct access from the living room to the bedrooms. But if there is separate circulation, there should be direct access from the bedrooms to the circulation and from the circulation to the living room (and there is no necessity for direct access from the bedrooms to the living room).

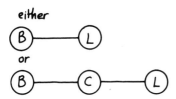

(f) Any circulation space must have direct access to the outside.

It is permissible to have direct access between rooms in addition to these minimum requirements. However, it is *not* permitted to have direct access to the bathroom either from the living room or from the kitchen/diner. Such direct relations between bathrooms and 'habitable' rooms are generally forbidden by building regulations in Britain, on hygienic grounds.

There is one final restriction on permitted arrangements in the plan. Every room (with the exception of any circulation space) must have at least one wall on the exterior, so as to allow for natural lighting and ventilation through windows. Thus a plan such as that shown in Figure 75, where the bathroom is completely in the interior, is unacceptable.

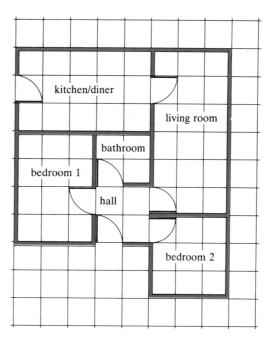

Figure 75   Inadmissible arrangement, because one room (the bathroom) is completely internal and cannot have a window

The functional diagram

Suppose for the moment that the plan does not contain a corridor or hall, then I can put together all the access requirements into a functional diagram as in Figure 76.

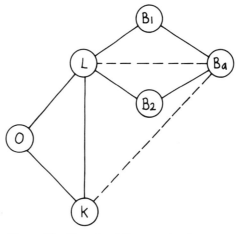

Figure 76   Functional diagram showing access requirements between rooms, in plans without a separate circulation space. Broken lines show forbidden access relations

The broken lines show the two forbidden access relations. One permissible set of access relations for plans containing a circulation space is shown in Figure 77(a), overleaf.

See how an approximate plan can be derived directly from the functional diagram, by drawing 'bubbles' for the rooms around each of the small circles (with the exception of the circle O for outside) such that adjacent bubbles touch, as in Figure 77(b). Of course these bubbles will then have to be 'squared up' into rectangular shapes of the specified sizes. Notice, however, that there are very many different ways in which the same functional diagram can be drawn, by moving the relative positions of the small circles, by turning parts of the diagram around, or by folding its branches over. Thus there are many distinct plans to which it can correspond.

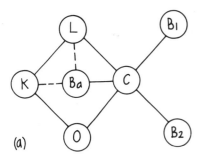

(a)

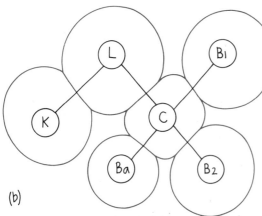

(b)

Figure 77 (a) Functional diagram showing access requirements between rooms, in a plan with a separate circulation space. Broken lines show forbidden access relations. (b) The diagram can be converted into a plan or plans where the rooms are approximated as bubbles

You might imagine that by putting such strict limitations on the shapes and sizes of rooms, as well as these requirements on the relations between the rooms, that the number of possible plans might be rather small. This, however, is not the case; I estimate that there are something over two million feasible arrangements just for those plans that have no circulation space, as well as many more if a hall or corridor is incorporated. Notice that I have set no requirements that the shape of the plan as a whole be a simple rectangle; and it is quite legitimate to have plans with irregular boundaries (so long as they lie on the grid), as in Figure 78.

Your job at this stage is therefore to try to find a plan in which the rooms conform to the specified limits on size and shape, and where the arrangement allows the doors to be placed where they satisfy all the required relations of access. You might go about this

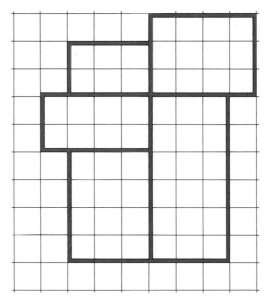

Figure 78   Plan with irregular perimeter

in various different ways. You could try sketching arrangements on squared paper, using the functional diagram as a guide.

Alternatively you could try cutting out rectangular pieces of card to the correct scale, to represent the rooms, and moving them about on the grid rather like jigsaw pieces. (Figure 79. Note that the room sizes and shapes shown in this figure are just for illustration and do not indicate the whole allowable range.)

I suggest that you spend a little time on this problem now. You should not find it too difficult to produce at least one and probably several arrangements that satisfy all the rules.

You should not decide finally on any particular plan at this point, however. You should read on to the end of this part, since there are several more considerations to take into account in choosing between different

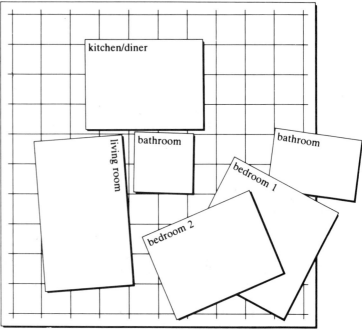

Figure 79   Trying out room arrangements with rectangular pieces of card

possible plans. With these in mind you can come back in due course and select some few arrangements for further detailed design and evaluation.

The aspects I refer to are:

the structural design of the house;

the arrangement of windows to provide day lighting;

the heating of the house, including the extent to which solar radiation can act as an 'incidental' source of heat in winter;

certain detailed aspects of the planning and layout of individual rooms, as affected by functional considerations and 'human factors';

finally, the cost of the house, both its cost of construction and the annual cost of heating.

Of course there are many other features of house design, perhaps as important or more important than these, that the architect would have to consider in any real design. These could include consideration of ventilation, of possible overheating in summer, of acoustics and sound insulation, of other services besides heating, such as electricity and water supply, of the views from windows, of various aesthetic aspects of the forms and spaces in the design, in fact the whole range of factors that have been already touched on in Part Two.

I have chosen to focus on just the few topics mentioned for three reasons: first, in order once again to simplify the exercise; second, because heating and structure are two of the most important *technological* aspects of house design, and this is, after all, a course about technology; third, because, as you will see, there are some interesting *interactions* between the demands of lighting and heating, structure and heating, and all three with room arrangement, and these in turn all have their effects on costs, both construction and running.

Structure of the house

You will already have learnt, from the discussion of structural principles in Section 10 'As safe as houses' and in *Structures and Materials*, that the way the structure of the average house works is difficult to define with precision. It is generally very much 'over-designed', in the sense that the structural members are (for other, quite good reasons) much larger than is strictly necessary to carry the imposed loads and to resist bending. In any case it is unusual to make detailed calculations for the structural design of small buildings such as houses, and instead the architect and builder rely on standard practices and rules of thumb.

It is nevertheless possible to say in very general terms that there is a relationship

between the *span* of some framed structure and its cost, so that the wider the unsupported horizontal span of a beam or floor slab is, the greater is the structural depth required, and the greater the cost. I have incorporated this general relation into this house design exercise by making some very simple rules about how the structure must be disposed. Remember that the roof of the house is to be flat. The construction is to be of timber, with a series of joists spanning in one direction between supporting walls, and for economic reasons no joist is to span more than 4 metres.

Once you have fixed on a particular room arrangement you will therefore need to go on and decide in which direction the different sections of the roof are to span and therefore which must be the load-bearing walls. For example, in the plan shown in Figure 80 the arrows indicate the directions in which the joists run; the walls shown as thick lines are the load-bearing walls. Notice that in no case are the joists longer than 4 metres. It is not a necessary requirement that the joists should all be parallel, though they are in this case.

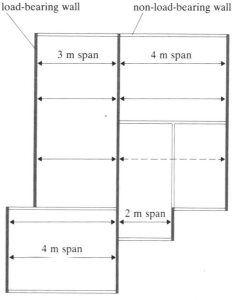

load-bearing wall   non-load-bearing wall

Figure 80   One possible way of arranging the roof structure of a five-room plan. Solid lines show load-bearing walls. Double lines show non-load-bearing walls. Arrows show the directions in which the various parts of the roof span

There must be load-bearing walls along the complete length of both sides of each section of roof, to carry the joists. In some cases it will be necessary to have openings in these walls for doors or windows, but such openings must not be too large or too many. You should arrange your plan so that there is no continuous opening in a load-bearing wall greater than 1 metre in width. You will see later that the range of available structural components allows for doors, windows and sections of wall that are all 1 metre wide.

This rule means in effect, therefore, that any window unit or door in a load-bearing wall must have solid 1 m wall units on either side. Notice that there is no such restriction, however, for doors or windows in walls that are not load-bearing. The doors should be assumed to have their own frames and not to require the support of a wall unit, necessarily, to hinge on. Doors and windows may be placed next to each other and it is quite permissible to have an entire 'window wall'.

There is one further structural rule: a door or window must not be placed at the end of a load-bearing wall in such a way that it leaves the corner of the roof unsupported. Figure 81 is an example of a permissible arrangement, while the arrangement in Figure 82 is not permissible.

When it comes to consideration of cost you will see that the cost of construction will be affected to some degree by the way in which you choose to arrange the structure. The cost

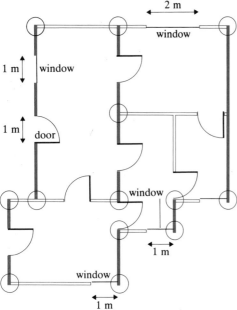

Figure 81 Permissible placing of openings in load-bearing walls. The corners of each part of the roof are all supported and no door or window opening is greater than 1 metre

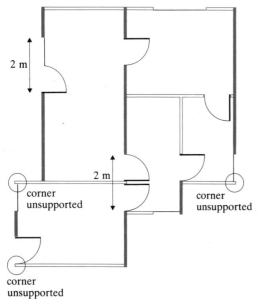

per square metre of a section of roof with 4 metre span is greater than that of 3 metre or 2 metre span. And the cost of load-bearing wall per unit length is taken to be greater than the cost of non-load-bearing wall.

Natural lighting

You should assume that it is required to have natural lighting in all the rooms of the house, with the possible exception of the circulation space. This lighting is to be provided by windows. Another possibility, since this is a single-storey building, would be rooflights, but that option is not included here. The windows can simultaneously serve to provide ventilation and views to the outside. As with structure, for houses it is unusual to make calculations of the levels of daylight provided by windows of different sizes and in different positions, and architects rely on precedent and experience. Such calculations might be made where precisely controlled levels of daylight are very important, such as in art galleries. Some elaborate mathematics is required and with building forms of any complexity it is virtually obligatory to use a computer for making the calculations. Alternatively, scale models can be employed.

Nevertheless, there are obviously lower limits on the sizes of windows, in relation to the areas and shapes of rooms, below which the lighting provided becomes inadequate, even if these limits are hard to specify with precision. For the sake of this exercise I have allowed for this by making a rough-and-ready rule that there should be not less than $0.5 \, m^2$ of window area for every $4 \, m^2$ of floor area in a given room. When you come to precise details of construction you will see that the range of 'components' from which the house is to be built allows for windows of three sizes: $0.5 \, m^2$, $1 \, m^2$ and $1.5 \, m^2$. The minimum areas of window for differently sized rooms are therefore:

up to $4 \, m^2$ floor area: $0.5 \, m^2$ minimum window area;

more than $4 \, m^2$, up to $8 \, m^2$ floor area: $1 \, m^2$ minimum window area;

more than $8 \, m^2$, up to $12 \, m^2$ floor area: $1.5 \, m^2$ minimum window area;

and so on.

Construction and costs of construction

As just mentioned, the construction of the house is assumed to be made up from a limited range of components of fixed size and physical properties, and at given costs. It is as though the house were prefabricated from factory-made sections; although the same principles would apply if it were a traditional construction of, say, brick and the

Figure 82 Some impermissible placings of openings in load-bearing walls. Corners of parts of the roof are unsupported and openings for doors and windows are greater than 1 metre

'components' simply an imaginary subdivision of the walls, roof, etc. into notional pieces for the purposes of calculation.

You need to consider the floor, the roof and the walls, as well as doors and windows. Roof and floor are divided up for the purposes of costing into units of 1 m², that is, they are assigned a cost per grid square covered. Note that the cost of roof area per square metre varies according to the span of the section in question and there are three different costs, one for spans of 4 m, one for spans of 3 m and one for spans of 2 m.

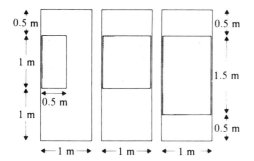

Figure 83
Wall units with large and small windows

The walls are divided into units which are 1 m wide and 2.5 m high (which is the height of the building). There are several different types of wall 'unit'. An external door unit incorporates a door and frame which together take up the complete unit. For windows there are three units, each incorporating a different sized window, as shown in Figure 83. The smallest has a window area of 0.5 m² and the largest 1.5 m².

A wall itself can be one of four types depending on whether it is an internal or external wall and whether it is load bearing or not. Only external walls can be insulated, and only load bearing walls can support a roof. Windows can only be incorporated into external walls. Doors can be included in external or internal walls; however, note that for the purposes of the heat and cost calculations the internal doors are counted as if they were standard internal wall units of the same type as the wall in which the door is situated. Also note that because the cost of window units is dominated by the cost of the window frame and glass no distinction is made between the cost of windows in load and non-load-bearing external walls.

Each of the wall building components is represented by a coloured strip which you will stick onto the tracing paper when assembling your plans. The colours used to represent the different components are set out in Table 2. Table 2 also shows the costs of the basic components, that is the costs without any insulation added. Adding insulation to any component will increase its cost.

The costs shown in Table 2 include all the associated costs of assembling and finishing the component in question. Thus totalling all the costs of all the building components will give a good estimate of the cost of erecting the house shell. However, there are many other costs that are involved in building a house. These include land costs, professional fees, wiring, plumbing, installing heating systems, decorating and so on. In the calculation of overall building costs these items are all lumped together in a single figure. They are added to the shell costs to provide a realistic estimate of the total building costs (in 1988 prices).

Table 2   Colour codes and costs of building components

	Colour code	Cost (1988 prices) (£/unit)
Walls		
external load bearing	orange	200
external non-load bearing	brown	175
internal load bearing	black	190
internal non-load bearing	red	165
Windows		
small (0.5 m²)	green/blue	300
medium (1.0 m²)	green	400
large (1.5 m²)	yellow	500
Doors		
external doors	blue	400
internal doors	black	
floors (per m²)	(squares)	45
Roofs		
2 m span (per m²)	(squares)	35
3 m span (per m²)	(squares)	50
4 m span (per m²)	(squares)	65

Heat loss calculations

Section 13 of Block 1 *Computing* sets out details of how to use the spreadsheets in order to complete the cost and heating calculations. There is also an audio tape session to introduce you to the spreadsheets. If you have not already studied these then now is the time to do so. This section of Block 1 *Computing* assumes that you have completed your study of the rest of the computing tributary and Block 1 *Heat*.

The heat loss calculations set out in the Heat Loss spreadsheet follow the procedures set out in Section 4 of Block 1 *Heat*. The fabric and ventilation losses for the house are worked out from the house dimensions and *U*-values. These are combined to give the specific loss, that is the rate of loss of heat from the house per 1 °C temperature difference. Next the internal and solar gains are evaluated. Notice that the solar gains depend both upon the window area and the level of glazing; double glazed windows admit less sunshine than single glazed windows (due to partial reflection from the glass). Instructions on how to include double glazed (or triple glazed) windows are included on the audio tape session. The average internal temperature inside the house is worked out from a formula that depends upon the specific loss and the house floor area. The formula used in this part of the spreadsheet has been derived from a more sophisticated model of house heating. It assumes that the house is heated to 21°C for 2 hours in the morning and 7 hours in the evening.

Once the average inside temperature has been evaluated, and the gains and specific loss, the base temperature can be worked out. The base temperature is then used in another formula to get the degree days. Finally, the heat required is the degree days multiplied by the specific loss multiplied by the number of seconds in a day (86 400). To work out how much fuel is required the heat requirement is divided by the proportion of the heat that is useful inside the house. This is taken as 70%. The annual heating cost is this quantity of fuel multiplied by the cost of gas, taken to be 0.36 p/MJ.

Your task in evaluating your design is to aim to minimize the combined total of the annual heating costs and the annual mortgage repayments. The mortgage repayments are worked out in the Building Cost spreadsheet using a formula; the calculation assumes a 10% rate of interest over a period of 25 years.

Your first plan

You are recommended to regard your first plan as a sort of trial run. It is only when you have *completed* the design and evaluation of one plan that you will really appreciate the interactions between all the constraints and requirements; so do not try to get the first one exactly right. Below are some of the options that you could consider in this first plan.

You might expect that making the plan as compact as possible will have the effect of reducing heat loss, by reducing the areas of external surfaces; but on the other hand, there might be some advantages to be gained by

having an elongated plan with several windows facing south, in order to increase solar heat gain.

Introducing extra windows will generally act to increase the rate of heat loss from the house, since even double-glazed windows are poorly insulating and have high *U*-values. On the other hand, if these windows face south, they may again have some counterbalancing advantage by admitting solar heat.

Although the floor and roof areas, and hence the capital costs of these elements, might be minimized by making the rooms all as small as possible, there might be ways in which a shorter perimeter and hence lower outside wall costs (and running costs) might be achieved by making some of the rooms larger than the given minima.

With the arrangement of the structure, the costs of the roof can be reduced by making spans shorter, but this may have other effects, possibly, in requiring more load-bearing walls (which are more expensive than non-load-bearing), or by making the plan less compact than it could otherwise be, thus affecting heating costs.

With these possibilities in mind, try choosing a specific plan that you think will be the best synthesis within all these conflicting factors, and work through the structural design, heat-loss calculations and costing in detail.

First use the note-taking skills that you have been learning, to go back through the preceding sections and to summarize all the various rules and requirements that have been specified. Then I suggest you work through the whole operation as follows:

1 Use the gridded site plan to lay out your design. Use the coloured adhesive strips to represent the different kinds of wall units, windows and doors. Table 2 specifies which colours correspond to which types of component. (Notice that small windows are denoted by a pair of colours: green/blue.) See Figure 84 for a sample plan laid out on the grid.

2 Check that the area and shape of each room lies between the specified limits.

3 Check that the placing of rooms and doors between rooms, as well as doors to the exterior, is such that all the access requirements in the functional diagram are fulfilled.

4 Check that the area of window provided in each room is not less than the specified amount in relation to floor area (i.e. at least 0.5 m² of window for each 4 m² of floor area).

5 When you have decided in which direction each part of the roof spans, check that this span is never greater than 4 m and that the roof is supported on the two sides by load-bearing walls. Check that there are no

continuous openings in these load-bearing walls wider than 1 m and check that the roof is nowhere unsupported at its corners.

6 Enter the details of your plan into the Data Entry spreadsheet and work out the total annual costs. Explore how these vary as you change the level of insulation on each element. You may also like to try moving windows around or changing their sizes since these are relatively easy changes to make. Keep notes of the changes in annual costs.

You may also find it useful to note down the total floor area of the design, and the total length of perimeter wall, since these will also provide useful points of comparison between alternative schemes.

Design strategy

Once you have decided on your first design and have worked out all the costs, you will probably be able to see some changes that could be made, which would result in a reduced cost. These might be fairly minor alterations. You might decide to alter the position or size of one room. You might decide to rearrange the structural layout, or move some of the windows and doors. Try to think of ways in which the *position* of a door or a window can have an effect on cost, without the total number or types of constructional components being changed. You might decide to put in, or to remove, some insulation.

Remember to check, for each new design you make, that all the various rules governing the structure, the lighting and the arrangement of rooms are still obeyed.

When you have finished with the evaluation of a particular plan it is a good idea to number the plan, change the title of the Data Entry spreadsheet and then save it on your student disk. Change the title of the frame to something like Version 1 or Plan 1 and then save it. If you want to go back to that spreadsheet later on and repeat or change some of the calculations, then you will have to change the name back to Data Entry since the name of the frame is referenced in the other spreadsheets (i.e. the heat loss calculation will look for the frame called Data Entry in order to find out the areas and U-values of the components). Remember to keep notes of the changes you make to plans and your reasons for trying different plans.

Rather than making small alterations to try to improve some already costed design, you might want to test some entirely different sort of plan: elongated instead of compact, with the rooms in a quite different configuration, or perhaps completely insulated instead of uninsulated. It might make sense to experiment with several very different design

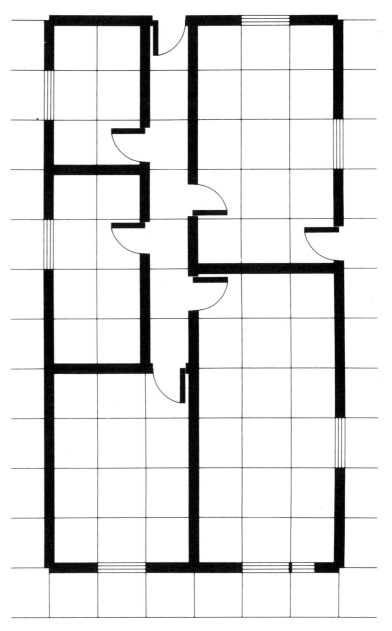

Figure 84 Sample plan laid out on site grid using adhesive strips

approaches at the beginning and compare them in general terms, *before* deciding to work on and refine one particular plan in detail.

So far the aim has been to try to achieve a plan for the house which has minimum cost. The sole criterion for evaluation has been financial. If you think you have reduced the cost as far as possible, or if you would simply now like to widen the scope of the exercise, then you can go on to consider some further aspects.

There are many other ways in which designs could be evaluated. Some of these *could* in principle involve making calculations, but of kinds that have not been explained in the block. Others rely on more qualitative methods of assessment.

In some cases a certain minimum level of performance has been built in to every design by virtue of the rules that were imposed on the 'generative' process. For example, the rule which specified the minimum area of window was intended to ensure (in a rough and ready way) that the levels of daylight in the rooms should be above some lower limit of acceptability. In reality, as you would imagine, there is a continuous relationship between the area of window in a room and the daylight level, so that the larger the window, the higher is the level. Obviously this relation is complicated by many factors, such as the orientation of the window, the presence of external obstructions, the internal geometry of the room and the tones and textures of the wall surfaces. It would have been theoretically possible to approach the natural lighting problem in very much the same way as the thermal performance has been treated, that is, by first generating an arrangement of rooms of various shapes and sizes and then working out the resulting daylight levels in those rooms.

There are two reasons why your design task was not organized in this way: first, because, as already mentioned, lighting calculations are very difficult, and second, because it is unusual for architects to work like this. Architects know in advance that windows of a certain size will be sufficient for the demands of lighting. In any case, daylight requirements in rooms are not all that critical: most domestic activities, with the exceptions of reading and sewing, can be carried on under a wide range of lighting conditions, and the size of windows in rooms can acceptably vary within very broad limits, as your own experience of different houses will confirm.

There are other factors that enter into the design of windows, since letting in daylight is by no means their sole function. They also serve to give views of the outside world, they can allow transmission of solar heat, they can be used to provide ventilation and they can be considered as formal elements in the aesthetic composition of the building facade. Architects will generally be thinking about several or all of these functions and how to arrive at a compromise between them.

There are many other such features of performance that will either not be worth calculating, or else impossible to calculate. Instead, architects use their judgement and experience to make choices between alternatives. Since they are working with drawings, and perhaps with physical models, architects must project themselves in imagination into the building that the drawings or models represent. They must look at the house from many different angles, both in a literal sense by making drawings of different parts and from different viewpoints,

and in a more metaphorical sense by thinking of the ways in which the house will be used, how people will move through it, how the furniture might be arranged and so on.

To do this for your own designs will be a much more open-ended process than was the calculation of cost, and one demanding greater imagination. Hence I am going to offer you only a set of suggestions, rather than definite procedures to follow, in the hope that you can expand or develop from these with your own ideas.

So far there has been no real client specified for the house, beyond the assumption for the purposes of calculating incidental heat gains that there are two adult occupants and no children. You might wish to change this assumption and to identify particular individuals (perhaps including yourself) for whom the house is specifically intended. It may follow that you would like to change the number and sizes of rooms or their required functional relations.

You might wish too to be more specific about the site of the house; for instance, you might imagine its position in relation to the street, to a garden, to neighbouring buildings, or to the landscape beyond.

Once you have made some decision about the client and site, then you can begin to elaborate and evaluate your designs further.

1 You can specify *furniture* and fittings for each of the rooms and show how they would be arranged. There is a printed card supplied depicting the plan views of various standard pieces of furniture, bathroom fittings, kitchen units, etc., which you can place under the site plan and trace off for this purpose. If you want to include other items, then you can draw these (at 1:50 scale) directly on the plan.

Think how the positions of the *doors* will affect the way in which people will walk through the house. In rooms with two doors there will be an effective 'corridor' along which people may be passing back and forth. The convention used for drawing doors on the adhesive labels shows the area in plan through which the door swings. The point of this is that it becomes immediately obvious from the plan if two doors would bang together when opened, or if sufficient space is provided to get into small rooms such as bathrooms. Remember that space must also be allowed for opening the doors of kitchen cabinets, refrigerators, cookers, etc.

2 You might find it useful to imagine the *pattern of activities* in different rooms over the course of a day, and how they will create requirements for particular furniture or for relations between rooms, rather as in the 'diary' illustrated in Figure 39. As well as thinking of routine events, think about the unusual occasion. You might be able to fit a

double bed in the bedroom, but can you get it there; can the removal people manoeuvre it in through the corridor? What about space for having a party? For sitting outside when it is sunny? What about arrangements when someone is ill in bed, or there are guests to stay?

3 Your choice of *site* will have a number of consequences. It may affect the arrangement of rooms in the plan, or how the whole house is oriented, so as to allow a front door to the street, say, or to give particular views from particular rooms. You will already have seen the effects of orientation on solar gain through the windows; but you might consider other effects of orientation.

If you have imagined neighbouring buildings or trees on the site, then these may have an effect in casting *shadows* over the house.

It is possible to work out the extent of the *view* from any point inside a room by drawing lines on the plan from that point passing out through the end-points of the window in question.

Where there are neighbouring buildings, this raises the question of *privacy*: will the neighbours be able to see in through the bathroom or bedroom windows?

4 The appearance of the house is only really possible to visualize with the aid of drawings. You might like to draw some elevations of the exterior of the house. Perhaps you would prefer on aesthetic grounds some different shapes and sizes of window from those shown in Figure 83.

As a result of all these assessments you may decide to make changes and go round the 'generate and test' cycle once again.

Whatever choices you make, whatever particular circumstances of site and surroundings you imagine, whatever particular tastes and requirements you invent for your client, be sure to note them down. In particular, be sure to state explicitly when you have decided to alter the previously established 'rules of the game', and in what way.

Finally you might have some criticisms of the general limitations which the 'kit of parts' approach as a whole has created. It is possible to change the details of construction or the values for costs etc., while still staying within the general discipline imposed, but of course it is not possible within this discipline to build anything but rectangular plans or, for example, to include pitched roofs. Such features would raise constructional and structural problems of new kinds. Still, you may have some general ideas about how these or other options could be incorporated and the exercise made more realistic and wider in scope.

13 Systems, modelling and design

In this final section of the mainstream I want to highlight the development of some of the main themes that will run right through the course. These themes – systems, modelling and design – were introduced in the *Introduction* and have been mentioned a few times during this block. Much of the development of these themes is implicit in what you have been reading and the main purpose of this summing up is to draw out the central ideas that have been covered.

In the last two sections you have seen how much of the material in this block can be drawn together to aid the process of designing a house. The design process itself is an intricate mixture of analysis, creativity and synthesis. In the design exercise you were asked to focus on the trade-off between just two aspects of a house, its building costs and heating. Architects have to consider a much wider range of trade-offs than this, many of them unquantifiable, for example, the overall external appearance of the house and how it 'fits' with its location; the views the occupants get from inside the house and how these can be improved by orientation of the house and landscaping. In many ways the quantifiable aspects of the design process are the easiest to deal with precisely because they can be quantified. However, there is no doubt that the secret to successful design involves capturing the non-quantifiable aspects and coming up with something creative and appealing – and there are examples of this in every walk of life. To some degree you were introduced to one example in Part One when looking at the wide ranges of 'homes' in different cultures. Each of those types corresponds to one successful solution to the design of a house – and each solution is geared to meeting the most binding local constraint, be it the availability of materials, the need for quick assembly or a way of providing a comfortable environment under difficult circumstances.

One of the difficulties with appreciating the process of design is that excellent designs always look obvious in retrospect. Indeed this could be regarded as a simple criterion for assessing excellence in design! So it is only by trying to put oneself in the shoes of the designer *before* a solution was found that one can begin to appreciate the nature of the design task.

Embedded within the overall activity of design are the functions of analysis and modelling. Earlier, in Section 11, I referred to the use of some systems ideas in aiding the process of analysis. There I emphasized the importance of being clear about the particular 'view' that was being taken of the situation and the advantage of clearly defining the boundary of each of the systems so identified. This topic will be developed further in Block 2. The business of selecting an appropriate system boundary will be developed in Block 3, where it will be shown that one's analysis of a situation can be dramatically altered by an apparently innocuous shift of the system boundary.

Which leaves modelling. This may be an area that has presented you with a few difficulties already since a wide range of models have been introduced and used in this block, ranging from abstract conceptual models (of heat) to diagrams and then to detailed computer models. These are all a long way from the conventional use of the term 'model' to mean a small scale representation of an object (as in 'model railways'). Indeed it may be difficult for you to see what all the things I have called 'models' have in common. Their common feature is to do with providing you with a representation of something that is simple enough to allow you to manipulate the relationships so as to either understand or predict what is happening.

The key ingredients in the last sentence are 'representation', 'simple' and 'manipulate'. All models are representations of something: the model railway is a representation of the real thing; our model of heat is a representation of what happens when things get hotter and colder; the spreadsheet model is a representation of the relationships between house insulation, climate and heating requirements. As representations they are useful in so far as they are able to extract the essence of the situation and leave behind what is irrelevant for your present purposes – and this is why to be useful models always have to be simplifications of the reality they represent.

The simplification must obviously not go so far as to lose any of the essential qualities or properties of what is being modelled – at least not in the circumstances under which the model is going to be used. Our model of heat grossly simplifies the relationship between thermal phenomena, fuels being burnt, solar radiation and the transfer of heat. However, for the circumstances in which we want to use the model these are all helpful simplifications – they leave behind complications that need not concern us in this context.

But in the context of Block 3, later in the course, the simplifications I have made here are too severe and have eliminated many of the phenomena which are of interest in Block 3, including the change of state of a substance and the conversion of energy from one form to another. So the model we find most appropriate here is no longer appropriate in Block 3.

Does this mean that the heat model is not 'right'? No, it does not mean that at all. Indeed it would be a mistake to try to apply the more complex energy model described in Block 3 to work out the heating requirements of a house; no heating engineer would dream of doing so because the more complex model brings in a whole range of considerations that are inappropriate to the business of calculating how much heat a house requires. So what is the 'right' model is something determined by the context in which it will be used; it's a matter of horses for courses.

The final characteristic of a model that I included in my description was that it enables you to 'manipulate' something. It may be that it provides a basis for describing a relationship; or that it provides a way of quantifying the process in detail, as in the case of the spreadsheet model used to calculate heating requirements and construction costs.

By the way did you notice that I used a model for calculating the construction costs? It is a very simple model based on the idea that things come in units with a fixed cost per unit. But of course this is a simplification of the reality. Anyone who has ever worked on a building site or had anything to do with getting materials for a major extension for a house knows that the idea of being able to know in advance how much of anything is needed is pie in the sky. All sorts of things go wrong between the architect's drawings and the final building. Some things are broken, some are lost, some details were not thought out correctly, delivered parts don't fit together (a well known axiom of Murphy's Law) and so on.

The 'model' I used for calculating the costs of construction completely ignored all these aspects of the reality. Instead it took the agreed current costs of building typical house elements – which are averages worked out over a number of sites and which take into account all these variations, at least on an average basis. So even in something as apparently simple as calculating the cost of building a house I have to use a model, and in using it I have to be aware of the approximations and simplifications it makes and have to check that these are consistent with the task for which I am using the model.

In this particular case I found that the conventional methods for calculating the costs of insulation were too crude to serve the purpose of the exercise, so I refined them somewhat.

So do you always have to use models? Well, in principle the answer is no: instead of operating on a simplified representation you could go to work on the real thing. Rather than use a model of how much it costs to build and heat your house design you could actually build the house, live in it and find out how much it actually costs to build and heat. But of course you would have only found out those costs under one particular set of circumstances; for example, the heating costs you observe will be for the particular weather you have during the year, which could be better or worse than average. But at least it would not be a model, it would be the real thing! With models, such as the heating calculation in the spreadsheet, regular exercises are carried out to check that the model does match with the reality fairly well. The check involves measuring the heating requirements of a large number of houses and then comparing these with the results of calculations made using the model.

Where discrepancies are found the model will be refined in some way (for example by being made less simplified), or its range of application may be re-defined to exclude the cases it cannot deal with. Most detailed engineering models, especially the quantitative ones, are checked in this way against what happens in practice. One of the most common challenges facing technologists is how to extend their models into new realms so that they can extend their range of practice further, be it building a bigger bridge, a faster computer, a taller building or a house that requires no heating. There is thus an intimate relationship between the process of building models and doing things for real – which is why modelling is one of the major themes of this course.

Let me now try to summarize some of the important points made in the study notes included in this block.

You need to find methods of efficient reading and note taking. These will be personal to you. The quicker you can develop such effective study methods, the easier it will be for you in the long run.

Reading skills

Use contents pages.

Try to anticipate what might appear in a particular section.

Read introductions and summaries carefully.

'Skim-read' and read pages 'out of order' when that suits your purpose.

Watch out for key terms and key sentences.

Look out for indications of how the author is organizing the material.

Try to distinguish main points from subpoints and both from examples.

Always make the most of diagrams and of other illustrations.

Note taking

Keep a list of key terms defined in your own words.

Take notes *for a purpose*.

Take notes in your own words wherever possible.

Make your notes personal.

Note taking should help you to *understand* what you read and keep you *active*.

Consider 'line', 'spray' and 'tree' note patterns.

Use diagrams etc. in your notes where this helps to save time or to make points clearer.

Checklist of objectives

After studying Block 1 *Home* you should be able to do the following:

1   Give a number of examples of simple traditional houses that demonstrate basic design principles.
(Section 1.)

2   Summarize the principal factors that help to explain the diversity of types of simple traditional houses.
(Section 2.)

3   Explain, with examples, how cultural norms can dominate in house design, leading to different designs even in the same physical environment, or to the adoption of designs that are not objectively suited to their physical environment.
(Section 5.)

4   Use the example of Le Corbusier's houses at Pessac to illustrate how people apparently prefer house designs that identify and express their own socio-cultural norms.
(Sections 5 and 6.)

5   Explain, with examples, how the pattern of family life and the house plan interact with one another.
(Sections 6 and 7.)

6   Describe and discuss a simple environmental 'comfort zone' defined in terms of air temperature and relative humidity.
(Section 8.)

7   Distinguish between 'purposive' and 'incidental' sources of space heating in a house.
(Section 8.)

8   Explain how climatic conditions might influence the choice of basic shape for a house.
(Section 8.)

9   Explain how the shape and orientation of a house influence the amount of solar heat it gains.
(Section 8.)

10   Explain how the choice of building materials affects the internal thermal environment of a house.
(Section 8.)

11   Distinguish between 'passive' and 'active' means of controlling the internal environment of a house.
(Section 9.)

12   Discuss, with the help of examples, how the provision of building services influences the plan of a house.
(Section 9.)

13   Give a brief explanation of how modern houses might be designed to be less dependent on mains services.
(Section 9.)

14   Explain how the choice of building materials affects the possible structural forms for a house.
(Section 10.)

15   List the properties of wood that help to make it such a useful building material.
(Section 10.)

16   Briefly outline the historical development of timber-framed house structures.
(Section 10.)

17   Explain how a house design can be seen as a synthesis of many factors: of many human requirements on the one hand and of many technological possibilities on the other.
(Sections 3 and 11.)

18   Make drawings of a house so as to emphasize selected aspects of its planning and design.
(Activities 1–6.)

19   Use an interaction matrix and functional diagrams to analyse and evaluate room relations in existing house plans and to help synthesize new plans.
(Section 7, Activity 3 and the design task.)

20   Given a limited design task, carry out the design cycle of 'generate and test' activities.
(Design task.)

21   Study effectively and efficiently by means of purposive reading and note taking.
(Study notes.)

Acknowledgements

Grateful acknowledgement is made to the following for permission to reproduce illustrations in this block:

Figure 1: Photographs by Jorgen Bitsch. Copyright National Geographic Society; *Figure 2*: Information Services, Canada House; *Figures 3 and 5*: Pitt Rivers Museum; *Figure 4*: USIS; *Figures 6 and 19*: Paul Popper Ltd; *Figure 7(a)*: Camera Press; *Figure 7(b)*: A. Rapoport; *Figures 8 and 15*: Courtesy of the American Museum of Natural History; *Figure 9*: *Radio Times* Hulton Picture Library; *Figure 10*: Museé de l'homme, photo: Griaule; *Figure 12*: from Griaule, *Conversations with Ogotemmeli*, International African Institute; *Figure 14*: from *Psychology of the House*, Editions de Seuil, 1972; *Figures 16(a) and (b), 17, 18, 21 and 22*: from P. Oliver, *Shelter and Society*, Barrie & Jenkins, a division of Century Hutchinson, 1969; *Figures 23 and 25(b)*: Architectural Association; *Figures 24, 25(a) and 27*: P. Boudon, *Lived-in Architecture*, Dunod and Lund Humphries, 1972; *Figure 26(a)*: photo. Stephen Shore from C. A. Jencks, *The Language of Post-modern Architecture*, Academy Editions, 1977; *Figure 26(b)*: from W. Laedrach, *Das bernische Stockli*, Verlag Paul Haupt Bern, 1951; *Figures 30–3*: from J. Wampler, *All their Own*, Oxford University Press, 1977; *Figures 34 and 35*: David Walker; *Figures 37(a) and (b)*: *The Architects Journal*; *Figure 38 (photos)*: Lucien Herve; *Figure 38 (illustration)*: from W. Boesiger, *Le Corbusier*, Verlag für Architektur 1972; *Figure 39*: from *Space in the Home*, HMSO. Reprinted by permission of the Controller of HMSO; *Figure 40*: reprinted from *The Geometry of Environment* by L. March and P. Steadman with kind permission of RIBA Publications Ltd, © 1971 RIBA publications; *Figures 42(a) and 53 (photo)*: Wayne Andrews; *Figure 44*: from V. Olgyay, *Design with Climate*, Copyright © 1963 Princeton University Press; *Figures 52(a), 70 and 71*: Hedrich Blessing; *Figures 52(c) and (d)*: from R. Banham, *The Architecture of the Well-Tempered Environment*, Architectural Press, 1969; *Figure 53 (illustration)*: from S. Cantacuzino, *Modern Houses of the World*, Studio Vista, 1970; *Figure 55*: from G. Boyle and P. Harper (eds.), *Radical Technology*, Wildwood House and Pantheon Books, a division of Random House, Inc., 1976; *Figure 56*: Zomeworks Corporation; *Figure 57*: Robert Vale; *Figure 59(a)*: John Donat; *Figure 60*: Keystone Press Agency; *Figures 65 and 66*: from A. S. Henderson, *The Family House in England*, J. M. Dent, 1964; *Figure 73*: Nigel Cross.